The Choice of Jesus Forsaken

The Choice of Jesus Forsaken

in the Theological Perspective of Chiara Lubich

Translated by Bill Hartnett

New City Press of the Focolare
www.newcitypress.com

Published in the United States by New City Press
202 Comforter Blvd., Hyde Park, NY 12538
www.newcitypress.com

©2015 New City Press (English Translation)
Translated by Bill Hartnett from the original Italian

LA SCELTA DI GESÙ ABBANDONATO
©2009 Città Nuova Editrice, Rome, Italy

Cover design by Leandro De Leon

Biblical citations are taken from the New Revised Standard Version
©1989 Division of Christian Education of the National Council of Churches of Christ
in the United States of America.

Library of Congress Cataloging-in-Publication Data

Gillet, Florence.
 [Scelta di Gesù Abbandonato. English]
 The choice of Jesus forsaken : in the theological perspective of Chiara Lubich / by Florence Gillet.
   pages cm
 Translation of: La Scelta di Gesù Abbandonato.
 Includes bibliographical references.
 Summary: «Chiara Lubich, Servant of God, discovered in Word and revelation, Jesus forsaken, and immediately decided to choose Him, that is, to love Jesus forsaken. The book shows that love for Him is an act of theological faith and as a consequence, it has ecclesial, sacramental, and social dimensions"-- Provided by publisher.
 ISBN 978-1-56548-506-8 (alk. paper)
 1. Jesus Christ--Crucifixion. 2. Trinity. 3. Lubich, Chiara, 1920-2008. 4. God (Christianity)--Love. I. Title.
 BT453.G5513 2015
 232'.4--dc23
                                    2015005420

In fact
nobody has had
greater trust than He;
forsaken by God,
He trusted in God;
forsaken by Love,
He entrusted Himself to Love.

Chiara Lubich,
The Cry

Contents

Preface by Piero Coda xi
Preface by Bishop Mulvey xv
Introduction 1

Part 1
Love for Jesus Forsaken According to Chiara Lubich

Premise: Jesus Forsaken is Situated Within
the Spirituality of Chiara Lubich 9

Chapter 1: A New and Enduring Discovery 13

    The Foundational Discovery of Jesus Forsaken 13

    Some Key Moments of Loving Response
    to the Love of Jesus Forsaken 17

Chapter 2: The Dynamic of Loving
Jesus Forsaken 29

    A Singular and Radical Choice 29

    Recognizing a Presence of Christ in Suffering Means
    Perceiving the Meaning in Reality 30

    From Embracing Him to Being Consumed in
    One With Him *(from Acceptance to Consummation)* .. 32

    Reliving Jesus Forsaken by Imitating His Love
    Creates a Community of Believers 33

Love for Jesus Forsaken is the Experience of the Triumphant Entry of God into the Soul, an Easter Event 36

Through Love for Jesus Forsaken the Risen Lord Radiates the Gifts of the Holy Spirit 40

As the Source of Happiness, Jesus Forsaken Asks that We Love Him with Pure Love 42

Loving Jesus Forsaken is a Mission 43

Mary Desolate, Icon of the One Who Loves Jesus Forsaken 44

Chapter 3: Faith to Understanding and Understanding to Faith: Who is Jesus Forsaken? 49

Having Made Himself Nothingness of Love, He is the Culmination of Revelation 49

By Becoming a Nothingness of Love, Jesus Forsaken is the Faith 50

His Nothingness Provides Some Understanding of Trinitarian Love 51

Because He Becomes Nothing Out of Love, He Receives the Gift of the Resurrection, the Fullness of Unity 52

Because He is Nothing, He is the New Creation 54

Conclusion 56

Part 2
How Humankind Relates to the Paschal Mystery in the New Testament

Chapter 4: In Paul's writings 59

Revelation of the Paschal Mystery in Paul 59

Gaining Access to the Paschal Mystery "Through Faith," Expressed in Being Reconciled with God 63

Faith and the Gift of the Spirit 66

Adhering to the Paschal Mystery Means Receiving Yourself from God's Hands 68

Living the Faith (Sharing in the Death and Resurrection of Christ), Builds Community 69

Faith Leads to Hope 71

Chapter 5: "Belief" in the Gospel of John 73

"Belief," Passing from Dialectic to Unity 75

Belief Places the Believer in Jesus' Hour, when He Returns to the Father 87

Mother of Jesus, Icon of Belief 94

Conclusion 95

Part 3
A Few Considerations on the Act of Faith

Chapter 6: The Act of Faith 103

   The Life of Faith Unfolds Upon a
      Landscape of Covenant and Love 103

   Faith Unfolds Upon a Landscape of
      Revelation and Knowledge 106

   Faith Unfolds Upon a Landscape of
      Divine Presence 108

   Faith Unfolds in a Sacramental and
      Especially Eucharistic Framework of
      Communion and Dialogue Among
      Brothers and Sisters 111

The Heart of the Gospel

I have always been thunderstruck by a very clear statement made by Chiara Lubich—I would say that inwardly it has turned me upside down—"Jesus is Jesus forsaken. Jesus forsaken is Jesus."

Contemporary theology has accustomed us to distinguish between the historical Jesus and the Christ of Easter (or of the faith), sometimes to the point of creating a gap between the two that becomes insurmountable or able to be overcome only by a leap of faith.

Chiara Lubich has a different perspective. It is certainly that of the great tradition of the church, but with a particular accent.

Indeed, Jesus is the entire Jesus, the Son of God made flesh who accomplishes the mission entrusted to him by the Father all the way to his death on the cross and his resurrection. Jesus is not simply the historical Jesus, but also the crucified and risen Jesus. These two are one, the same Jesus.

The powerful novelty, the decisive novelty—and at the same time solidly anchored in the New Testament and the tradition—is that this entire Jesus is totally unfolded, and therefore finds the center of his full revelation in Jesus forsaken. The abandonment reveals the deep and radical "who is" of Jesus, and therefore the hyphen between Jesus before the Pasch and Jesus after the Pasch. In and through the abandonment, Jesus enters into the resurrection. He is the risen One, and he introduces us together with him into the bosom of the Father.

As a sign of persevering discipleship, Florence Gillet guides us into this intuition as she opens up the very heart of the gospel to us. With vivid and peaceful theological intelligence, that intelligence that is love, she nourishes our life while nourishing our thought.

The fact is that if "Jesus is Jesus Forsaken," that is, the Son who entrusts himself to the Father, without residuals and conditions, in the act in which the Father seems to hide the name of Abba in the most cruel and darkest trial—if Jesus is this, then our faith in him is a partaking, through grace, intimately, in the very event of his abandonment. Our faith is carrying within us the faith of the abandoned One in the occupations of each day.

Thus showing us today what Christianity is and has to be. Especially today! Beginning with this re-reading of the Christian faith of the New Testament with simple eyes, we are able to scrutinize in the Spirit who has been given, the abyss of God's love; and from there, men and women, and the things of the world and of history.

Therefore, a precious gift has been given to us in these pages. It is at the same time a delicate and powerful gift. It is a gift—I would like to underscore—that has matured by the involvement, with trust and generosity, of the work of a group of theologians, women and men, laity and presbytery, Christians of different Churches and countries. They formed part of the Abba School[1] that Chiara wished to have at her side.

---

1. In 1992, the noted German theologian Klaus Hemmerle urged Lubich to begin reexamining her mystical writings and opening them to study. She formed an interdisciplinary study group to meet with her in this task that eventually expanded and became known as the Abba School. Some years after its founding, scholars in all fields of

This book is a first. It is the promise of an unobtrusive and fascinating theology, academically rigorous but not inaccessible, silhouetted but welcoming; something that, even in theology, spreads the fragrance of Mary.

Piero Coda
Professor of Theology,
Sofia University Institute

---

study from around the world were invited to meet in Rome on a regular basis to discuss the work of the Abba School in a broader venue.

To Follow Jesus Today

Clear definitions give direction to one's life. In order to follow Jesus today we need to understand who he is and accordingly respond to his call to discipleship and mission. Jesus himself wanted to clarify who he was for his disciples. "Jesus and his disciples set out for the villages of Caesarea Philippi. Along the way he asked his disciples, 'Who do people say that I am?' They said in reply, 'John the Baptist, others Elijah, still others one of the prophets.' He asked them, 'But who do you say that I am?' Peter said to him in reply, 'You are the Christ'" (Mark 8:27–28).

As then so now, the Holy Spirit continues to guide us to a clear understanding of who Jesus is. The gospels present many portrayals of Jesus: the one who heals, who forgives, who teaches, etc. With these being so familiar to people, it might seem strange to many to discern the "real" Jesus in the moment of his most extreme, personal and agonizing suffering. And yet that was the case for Chiara Lubich, when in 1944 she affirms Jesus as her "Ideal" in the moment he cried out on the cross to the Father, "My God, My God why have your forsaken me?"

The experience of being forsaken by the Father on the cross was presented to her as the highest point of Jesus' suffering. From that she determined that if that was the moment of his extreme suffering then it too was the uppermost expression of his love: "If that was the moment he suffered the most, then that was the moment he loved the most." For her and for those who have followed her spirituality through the Focolare Movement (Work of Mary) Jesus forsaken seen and loved in every personal and universal suffering is the transforming grace of the Paschal Mystery. In 1962 she wrote this about Jesus forsaken:

> So that we might have Light, you ceased to see.
> So that we might have union, you experienced separation from the Father.
> So that we might possess wisdom, you made yourself "ignorance."
> So that we might be clothed with innocence, you made yourself "sin."
> So that God might be in us, you felt him far from you.[2]

For Chiara Lubich and for those who are part of the Work of Mary, Jesus' historical presence and mission as well as his glorious resurrection intersect and are accomplished in the Forsaken Christ. The historical Jesus, one with humanity in all things but sin, cries out in filial faith to the Father in his intense moment of suffering and finding the Father's silence as the only response, gives himself over in total trust to the Father's love: "Father, into your hands I commend my spirit" (Luke 23:46).

When Chiara writes that "Jesus is Jesus Forsaken and Jesus Forsaken is Jesus" it is not merely a statement of theology for her but an intense truth that she has verified in her own life through a daily encounter with suffering as his presence—her "only Good."

In this book, Florence Gillet unfolds for us in theological terms an understanding of this profound mystery of Jesus — the highest manifestation of God's love and

---

2. Chiara Lubich, *Essential Writings* (Hyde Park, NY: New City Press, 2007), 94.

mercy. May Mary, Mother of the Incarnate Word, who at the foot of the cross witnessed the transforming mystery of suffering into Love, accompany the reader to a greater understanding of who Jesus is and to a faithful love for the Redeemer who endured all things for the salvation of all.

Bishop Michael Mulvey,
Corpus Christi, Texas

Introduction

Humanity has always sought to resolve the great problem of suffering, be it through anthropology, religion, literature, or philosophy. The Christian response to that problem, however, is not a technique but a person: the crucified and risen Christ in the moment of his passing from the greatest suffering, shame, and dehumanization to ultimate human fulfillment, resurrection, and the eternal life. It is Christ in his paschal mystery, the heart of the Christian faith for those called the New Testament "believers."

Every spirituality that has blossomed in the Church down through the centuries has addressed the paschal mystery. Like the others, the Focolare Movement has its own approach, which can be summed up in a name: *Jesus forsaken*. Together with unity, Jesus forsaken is the hallmark of the charism bestowed on Chiara Lubich in 1943. Like the paschal mystery itself, it can never be comprehended fully, but will always be examined and understood more deeply.

Many figures, especially Chiara Lubich, have written extensively on Jesus forsaken. Jesus forsaken is better examined, however, through the lives of people who have striven to live out the paschal mystery—Jesus forsaken and unity—putting it into effect, building up a work of God that ultimately is nothing other than the people themselves. According to Chiara Lubich, the Focolare Movement (officially called "The Work of Mary" by the Church)

1

"is what it is thanks to Jesus forsaken, its founder."[1] As with the primitive "missionary church," the Movement's success in spreading throughout the world can be attributed to living out the kerygma of the faith. "We can never insist enough on the fundamental importance of Jesus forsaken: "Stay with Chiara Lubich's first intuition," urged Hans Urs von Balthasar, "Jesus forsaken!"[2]

Understanding how the store of faith has produced Jesus forsaken, the Word of God, is the subject of much Christological and Trinitarian research, study, and reflection. But to any member of the Focolare Movement, Jesus forsaken signifies mainly love for Him and life through Him. Chiara's very first response to the Word/revelation of Jesus forsaken was, without any further reflection, *to choose Jesus forsaken, to love Jesus forsaken*, a choice that the General Statutes of the Work of Mary state clearly: "In their efforts to bring about unity, the members of the Work of Mary... *have a preferential love toward Jesus forsaken, and they strive to live Jesus forsaken* who in the culminating moment of his passion cried out: 'My God, my God, why have you forsaken me?' (Mk 15:34; Mt. 27:46) and became the artificer and way to unity for men and women with God and with each other" (Art. 8).

What does love for Jesus forsaken entail? What place should it have in the practice of the Christian life? Is it a form of devotion, a kind of asceticism, a virtuous activity, a practice, merely a technique? It is far more than any of these because "love for Jesus forsaken" must be examined from the perspective of theological anthropology—what

---

1. Chiara Lubich, *The Cry* (Hyde Park, NY: New City Press, 2001), 85.
2. Chiara Lubich, *Costruendo il "castello esteriore"* (Rome: Città Nuova, 2002), 65. Editor's translation. All other references from non-English language sources have been translated by the editor.

it means to be a human being in relationship to God. — as an example of what it means to believe. The purpose of this book is to show that love for Jesus forsaken is an act of theological faith; as a consequence, it has ecclesial, sacramental, and social dimensions.

The concept of faith presented in the New Testament corresponds closely with the complex reality contained in the expression "love for Jesus forsaken." Likewise, love for Jesus forsaken constitutes a veritable testing ground, a way of translating into real life the various aspects of faith presented in Scripture and deepening them.

The concept of faith is central to the New Testament; Christians are defined simply as "believers." They are believers before being witnesses, preachers, philanthropists, before being brothers and sisters. Faith is more central to the New Testament than love. The word *faith* is used 259 times; the word *believe* is used 222 times. Moreover, according to Paul, it is by faith that one is saved, justified, and made an heir. According to John, a believer has purification, adoption as a son or daughter, and eternal life.

Nevertheless, Christians of the twenty-first century still face a few questions. Are salvation, justification, eternal life, adoption as sons and daughters of God merely matters of faith to be enjoyed not in this life but only in the next? Are they all the objects of a hope projected into some eschatological future? Or, rather, are they already here-and-now things that we can possess and that can have an effect on social and ecclesial life? Is there a place where salvation and justification are achieved? Where is it? And if it does exist, why do we not experience it?

Where do we see this "work of God," according to John the only one worth doing, which consists in "believing in the only begotten Son" (see Jn 6:29)? Does this work remain hidden from human beings, to be revealed only in the next life, or does it have an effect on their lives in the here and now? These questions can be answered because faith allows us to experience eternal life already now. It is possible because we have been adopted as God's sons and daughters. This answer is not theoretical, but grounded in actual experience: love for Jesus forsaken as Chiara understood it. To members of the Focolare Movement, saying that love for Jesus forsaken is a saving act of faith may sound paradoxical. They would be puzzled by or even disagree with saying that Jesus forsaken as understood by Chiara is an act of faith. They would insist that it is a matter not of faith, but love! Chiara teaches her followers that Jesus forsaken is her style of love, a love whose goal is building unity and the Church, virtue and holiness. Jesus forsaken is their model, the one they must console, and they are his vineyard. They do not consider him to be their model in faith. Does such a claim, however, diverge from the authentic thinking of the founder?

Love for Jesus forsaken indeed does imply an authentic act of faith and makes evident many of the elements contained in faith's complex richness. Loving Jesus forsaken sheds light on the nature of faith; doing so can be considered a model of living faith. Such love is the exemplar of the act of faith because in it come about salvation and justification.

To show how love for Jesus forsaken and the act of faith are connected, I will first examine what love of Jesus forsaken consists in according to Chiara, highlighting the many aspects contained in this complex experience. Indeed, love for Jesus forsaken is something to be learned. Love for Jesus forsaken is a full sharing in the mystery of Christ, that is, the paschal mystery understood as incarnation, passion, death, resurrection, ascension, and Pentecost; therefore it is faith. I will discuss how a Christian participates in the mystery of Christ, based on the work of two New Testament writers: St. Paul and St. John. In light of this discussion, in the third and final section, I will offer some further considerations on the act of faith.

Part I

LOVE FOR JESUS FORSAKEN ACCORDING TO CHIARA LUBICH

Premise

Jesus Forsaken is Situated Within the Spirituality of Chiara Lubich

Love for Jesus forsaken is a journey. Those who set out upon it place themselves at the very heart of Revelation, at the very heart of the Christian experience. We must begin, however, by reiterating that Jesus forsaken is but one aspect of Chiara's spirituality; isolating it from the others would deform that aspect as well as the entire spirituality. It would be useful, therefore, to begin by explaining the place of Jesus forsaken within her spirituality.

The elements of this spirituality flow one from the other in logical sequence. None can be omitted without deforming the whole. Chiara did not invent these elements sitting at a desk; rather, they were born from a light and, I am not afraid to say, from a sort of revelation of the Spirit that corresponds deeply with *the* Revelation of which the Church is the sole depository. These elements mark foundational moments — at times sudden, even impetuous — or else they are answers questions that she, certainly prompted by God, had expressed in prayer. Chiara is first of all a witness to a "light" that God gave to her also for us, a light that places us in a posture of deep listening to the Spirit. With her entire being she responded to this light with a "yes" pronounced from the depths of her heart, a "yes" she repeated throughout her life. But this gift of God also entailed that she immediately communicate what she had understood to the people around her.

Chiara, the receptacle of a gift of God that she transmits to us, is therefore a master of the Christian life and of Christian light. This gift is so strong that to express herself she sometimes is forced to give new meaning to existing words or to invent a new vocabulary. The greater the gift of God, the more fragile and inadequate the vessel that contains it; Chiara was well aware of this: *I play a music that was written in Heaven; I'm but a small paintbrush in the hands of an artist.* As a woman in the pre-conciliar Church in Italy, the vessel that contained this great charism was considered quite fragile indeed. Yet she bore within many prophetic elements later to be transmitted through her life and her words.

Chiara uses the word *ideal* to identify her particular collection of gifts, light, human response, knowledge of the faith, wisdom, and life. This word contains many meanings. It signifies God who must be loved above all things and known through his Word and in his will. It is Jesus, the Word Incarnate, life model who is followed by drawing on the gospel, being another Jesus, and seeing Jesus in everyone. It is the Trinity, its dynamic of love re-lived by us in our interpersonal relationships. It is the Church. Thus the mystery of God becomes the very path for responding to God, the path of life and love that passes through the brother and sister. This is all contained in the word *ideal.*

Chiara's ideal, which is Christocentric and ecclesial, begins from Christ's intimate relationship with the Father and, in particular, two of Christ's prayers to the Father. The first that Chiara "discovered" was Jesus' cry to the Father, which is the subject of this book. The second, for which she gave every ounce of her strength, was the prayer called the "testament" of Jesus, the prayer for unity that Chiara sums up in the Latin phrase *Ut omnes* (that all [be one]) (see Jn 17:21).

The key points of Chiara's spirituality include: Godlove; the will of God; the life of the Word of God; love of neighbor; the new commandment of Jesus; Eucharist; unity as the Father's gift in response to Jesus' prayer; Jesus forsaken, who by being relived is the key to realizing unity; Mary, Mother of Unity; the Church as communion; the Holy Spirit. These eleven cardinal points of the spirituality stem from and aim at a twelfth: Jesus in the midst (see Mt 18:20). Chiara's spirituality is collective. The General Statutes of the Work of Mary begin with a premise, the "norm of norms": Jesus in the midst of his disciples. Even Jesus forsaken, who is so central to the spirituality, must always be seen in light of this premise. Mutual charity lies at the basis of the members' life, making unity possible and bringing the presence of Jesus into the collectivity. Jesus in the midst is the "norm of norms, the premise to every other rule."[3]

Chiara's experience regarding Jesus forsaken is interwoven with her life. To speak of him is to speak of the meaning of life, the soul of her existence, an ineffable reality. Jesus forsaken is often the first thing that fascinates those who know and live this spirituality, the only one, the rock upon which they have built their lives.

Chiara's life, like every mystery of love, transcends words; nevertheless, it is necessary to examine it carefully, scrutinizing the extensive material that is available. During the last ten years of her life, Chiara reflected on her own

---

3. *General Statutes of the Work of Mary* (New York: Focolare Movement, 2008), 13.

experience and on the life of the Focolare Movement by analyzing and commenting on the "early times." She realized the importance of those "early times" in coming to understand the authenticity of God's gift. To capture that original intuition, I will use Chiara's own words, both texts from those early times and some more recent reflections.

The event from which everything concerning Jesus forsaken flows is her discovery of him and subsequent decision to choose him. The *story* of her love for Jesus forsaken, its genesis and some key moments, makes it clear that on God's part this love is a revelation, a saving presence, a resurrection; on the individual's part, a loving response. Revelation, human response, and salvation constitute the dynamic of love for Jesus forsaken. For Chiara, Jesus forsaken is in himself the revelation of God, a saving presence, and the fullness of God's response in a new creation.

Chapter 1

A NEW AND ENDURING DISCOVERY

The foundational discovery of Jesus Forsaken

The story of the *discovery* of Jesus forsaken is well known in the Focolare Movement. In her book, *Jesus: The Heart of His Message*, Chiara Lubich allows her companion Dori Zamboni to tell what happened.

> We went in search of the poor and it was probably from them that I caught an infection on my face. I was covered with sores. The medicines I took did not halt the disease. But, with my face appropriately protected, I kept on going to Mass and to our Saturday meetings.
>
> It was cold, and to go outside under such conditions could have been bad for me. Since my family would not let me go out, Chiara asked a Capuchin priest to bring me Communion. While I was making my thanksgiving after receiving the Eucharist, the priest asked Chiara what in her opinion was the moment of Jesus' greatest suffering during his passion. She replied she had always heard that it was the pain he felt in the Garden of Gethsemane. Then the priest remarked: "But I believe, rather, that it was what he felt on the

cross, when he cried out: 'My God, my God, why have you forsaken me?'" (Mt 47:26).

As soon as the priest left, I turned to Chiara. Having overheard their conversation, I felt sure she would give me an explanation. Instead, she said: "If Jesus' greatest pain was his abandonment by his Father, we will choose him as our Ideal and that is the way we will follow him."

At that moment, in my mind and imagination, I became convinced that our Ideal was the Jesus of the contorted face crying out to the Father. And my poor facial sores, which I saw as shadows of his pain, were a joy to me, because they made me resemble him a little. From that day on, Chiara spoke to me often, in fact constantly, of Jesus forsaken. He was the living personality in our lives.[4]

At least four elements can be highlighted in Dori's account of the discovery of Jesus forsaken and Chiara's decisive adherence to him.

First, this incident took place at a particular time and place: Dori's house, Trent, January 24, 1944. This date marks a turning point, one of those memorable events in which even the tiniest details remain impressed on the mind. All of these details seem important; taken together they form a portrait, express a meaning.

It is important to note that at first, a word is proclaimed that appears "credible" even though it challenges an idea received from the Church. Chiara explains this in her book, *The Cry*. "The opinion among Christians at that time

---

4. Chiara Lubich, *Jesus: The Heart of His Message* (Hyde Park, NY: New City Press, 1985), 45–46.

placed it, rather, in the suffering of Gethsemane. But having great faith in the words of the priest as a minister of Christ, we believed the suffering of the forsakenness to be the greatest."[5] She uses the word *believed* inasmuch as she considered it to be the Word of God (through the priest). The "content" of this word, Christ abandoned by the Father, is *accepted* because he is the Word of God.

Secondly, Chiara hears and then actively welcomes the revelation. She chooses Jesus forsaken and immediately involves Dori as if they were chosen for a mission: "We will choose him as our ideal and that is the way we will follow him."[6] Jesus forsaken became the main personage in their lives. Moreover, Chiara realizes that her loving response to Jesus forsaken is God's gift. She states: "Then you showed me where to find you. 'Under the cross,' you told me, 'under every cross is where I am. Embrace it and you will find me.' You told me many times and I do not remember all the objections I offered. But you finally convinced me."[7]

Thirdly, *Jesus forsaken* is a term in which, for the mentality of a young Catholic woman of the 1940's, two apparently contradictory words are juxtaposed. How could Jesus, the second Person of the Holy Trinity, be forsaken by God? Chiara transcends this contradiction and, in obedience to the Word she has *receive,* chooses him. This choice leads her to a deeper understanding and revelation of God's love. She intuits a certain presence of God in suffering: every suffering is like a shadow of his suffering. Dori says it very clearly: "[T]hose miserly wounds on my own face... seemed to be a shadow of his pain." Furthermore, she immedi-

---

5. Lubich, *The Cry*, 38.
6. Lubich, *Jesus: The Heart of His Message*, 46.
7. Chiara Lubich, *Essential Writings* (Hyde Park, NY: New City Press, 2007), 56.

ately recognizes in Jesus forsaken the ultimate revelation of God-Love. She had already made the discovery that God is only love, but now she comprehends the love and the abandonment. Love reaches all the way to the abandonment.

The discovery of Jesus forsaken is inseparable from the discovery that at this very moment Jesus reveals his greatest love: Chiara *immediately* contemplated in him "the summit of his love, because it was the summit of his pain. In fact, Jesus forsaken reveals all the love of a God."[8] In a letter composed on January 30, 1944, one week after the encounter with Jesus forsaken she writes: "You will be the recipient of joys, you will be the recipient of pain and of anguish.... But if you only make an effort to see Jesus in the way I have presented him to you, in the culmination of his pain, which is the culmination of his love."[9]

Finally, the experience of recognizing Jesus forsaken in suffering becomes a source of joy because they became one with Christ. Dori states: "Those ...wounds ...gave me joy because they made me a bit like him."

This, then, is the dynamic of discovering Jesus forsaken: revelation on God's part; acceptance of the revelation on Chiara's part; awareness (which is a subsequent revelation) of a certain hidden yet real presence of God beneath every suffering; awareness of an attitude of endless love in God, and a sense of fullness, peace, joy, and salvation.

The foundational moment that occurred in Dori's home marked the beginning of a journey in which Chiara repeated her initial "yes" over and over again in countless different ways. Each of these yeses marked a new and deepening understanding of Jesus forsaken. Indeed, for the light that dazzled Chiara to be incarnated little by little in her and

---

8. Lubich, *Jesus: The Heart of His Message*, 52.
9. Ibid.

in her followers and transform every fiber of their being, a lifetime of vicissitudes was necessary—many sorrows, temptations, and unforeseen events. All of this made her personal response to Jesus forsaken more real and radical. We shall also see how these events and subsequent yeses reflect a dynamic of revelation, acceptance and new awareness of God's presence and love.

Some key moments of loving response to the love of Jesus Forsaken

a) Between Jesus Forsaken and Jesus Forsaken (Summer 1949)

Between January 1944 and the summer of 1949, the life of love for Jesus forsaken grew. The summer of 1949, a period when a "blaze of light dazzled us,"[10] was preceded by an intense life of love for Jesus forsaken. During the course of those years Jesus forsaken became more and more Chiara's *everything*: "In Jesus forsaken there were all sufferings, all loves, all virtues, all sins (since He had made Himself 'sin') and in Him we all found ourselves in every instant of our lives."[11]

> In that cry He appeared to us as suffering and love together. He had made Himself "sin" for us sinners, rebellion, division, excommunication, and so forth, out of love. I don't know how to link these two terms: love and suffering that in Jesus forsaken appeared to us to be a single thing, so that one would not exist without the other. By

---

10. Lubich, *Essential Writings*, 315.
11. Chiara Lubich, "Paradise '49," *Claritas: Journal of Dialogue and Culture*, 1, 1 (2012), http://docs.lib.purdue.edu/claritas/vol1/iss1/3. Published after her death, this passage dates back to 1961, when Chiara recalls the content of that special experience of summer 1949.

> living Jesus forsaken we had come to understand that He had made Himself nothing and that in this nothingness was our life. To be like Him out of love for Him, that nothingness that we really are. We, nothing, He all.[12]

The life of love for Jesus forsaken had made her realize that his life could be summed up in his *becoming nothing* and that her life had to correspond to his. It has to be the nothingness that she actually was.

During that summer of light and revelations from God, the Christian life was revealed to Chiara Lubich and her companions in a way that "appeared totally new" and in which they understood "many truths of the faith,"[13] played out on a landscape that God had been prepared through their loving and reliving Jesus forsaken to the point of being nothing. The entry into that period of light is also linked to love for Jesus forsaken. It began with Chiara's suggestion to Igino Giordani (known in the Movement as Foco) that they ask Jesus to connect their souls in unity as he knew it should be. She said to him:

> You know my life: I am nothing. I want to live, in fact, as Jesus Forsaken who made Himself completely nothing. You too are nothing because you live in the same manner.
>
> So then, tomorrow… to Jesus Eucharist who will come into my heart, as in an empty chalice, I will say: "On the nothingness of me, please may you make a pact of unity with Jesus Eucharist in the heart of Foco. And do things, Jesus, such that what comes out is the bond between us that you

---

12. Ibid.
13. Lubich, *The Cry*, 60.

have in mind." Then I added, and you Foco, do the same.[14]

Chiara describes the two-month period that followed: "Our experience was so powerful, it made us think life would always be like that: light and heaven. But what followed instead was the reality of everyday life. In that rude awakening, finding ourselves still on this earth, the only thing that gave us the strength to go on living was Jesus forsaken who was everywhere in this world that we had to love, which is as it is simply because it is not Heaven."

She continues: "And in a second choice, more conscious and aware of the One who had called us to follow after him, that well-known decision just flowed from my soul: I have only one Spouse on the earth: Jesus forsaken. I have no other God outside of Him. In Him is all of Heaven with the Trinity and all of the earth with Humanity. Therefore [what is] His is mine and nothing else. His is the universal Suffering and therefore [it is] mine."[15]

The period of light, known as *Paradise '49*, is therefore set between two great acts of love toward Jesus forsaken: the choice of being nothing at the beginning of the summer, after the intuition of the link between love and suffering in Jesus forsaken and sealed in the pact based on the nothingness of each person; and the declaration of exclusive and preferential love toward Jesus forsaken, leaving behind the Paradise they had experienced for two months. They did it only out of love for him, to seek only him back in this world.

---

14. Chiara Lubich, "The Pact," *Claritas: Journal of Dialogue and Culture*, 2: 1 (March 2013), 4, http://docs.lib.purdue.edu/claritas/vol2/iss1/3/.
15. Lubich, *The Cry*, 61. This passage is dated September 20, 1949. Chiara gives another version of her new "yes" to Jesus forsaken, leaving the summer of 1949, in *Paradiso '49*, 296.

b) Going beyond the wound in order to be Mary (December 1957)

Another important experience is known as *going beyond the wound*.[16] In 1957 Chiara Lubich went through a period of spiritual and physical trials so profound that she managed to live through them only by "never ceasing to look to Jesus forsaken, to the wound of his abandonment."[17] One day, she recounts, she felt urged to ask Jesus why "He had not found a way to also leave His Mother on earth, for us [who are] so in need of her help in the journey of life." She continues:

> In the silence, Jesus seemed to answer me from the tabernacle: "I have not left her because I want to see her again in you. Even if you are not immaculate, my love will virginize you; and you, all of you, will open your arms and hearts as mothers of humanity, which, as in times past, thirsts for God and for his mother. It is you who now must soothe pains, soothe wounds, dry tears. Sing her litanies and strive to mirror yourself in them."
>
> It was a moment when God re-emphasized in our hearts the conviction that the Work of Mary had to be nothing other than a mystical presence of Mary.[18]

Once again, Chiara's love for Jesus forsaken reaches a new level through a haunting pain, lived out in love. You need to comprehend, enter into the wound and pass beyond. This means "to embrace Jesus forsaken totally and find

---

16. Recounted in: Chiara Lubich, *Mary The Transparency of God* (Hyde Park, NY: New City Press, 2003), 37.
17. Ibid.
18. Ibid.

yourself beyond pain, in love."[19] Corresponding to this new love is a new understanding, a new revelation. She herself acknowledges that "we felt like we were contemplating the immense love which God has poured out over the world. It is in fact from the pain of the Crucified One, reaching its climax in that cry, that redemption comes, with sanctification and deification. 'Beyond the wound' we understood truly what love is; we were consumed by love and shared in its light: the light of Love. This was one way to express the vocation we felt to pass through abandonment in order to find God, who is Love."[20]

c) The experience of "The Feast" (Paris, January 1, 1959)

On December 31, 1958, Chiara Lubich went to Paris to visit a focolare house that had just been opened there. For some time she had been repeating a prayer that seemed to rise from her heart: "Grant that I may die rather than not welcome you crucified and love you forsaken."[21] But on that last day of the year, a day when people took stock of their lives and made resolutions, Chiara's prayer was more intense. She asked God for "an increase" of love: "Lord," she said, "grant that I may give a new tone to my life."[22] She put herself before God, as if before a teacher, "listening" to her charism: "Make me to know your ways, O Lord; teach me your paths" (Ps 25:4). And she returned to her first

---

19. Lubich, *Unity and Jesus Forsaken*, 72.
20. Ibid.
21. *Esperienze*, a collection of experiences previously published in *Città Nuova* magazine (Rome: Città Nuova, 1959), 216. The article is published under a pen name.
22. Ibid.

intuition: Jesus forsaken. Indeed, she could not live outside this illumination (see Heb 10:32).

On New Year's Day, during thanksgiving after Holy Communion, the prayer "Grant that I may die" died on her lips; it seemed to have died out. "What?" she wondered, "A love that forces, that struggles? No, love is spontaneous and free; a heart in love cannot but love." And here she found her light and firm purpose. "Oh, yes, Lord. I've understood! Whenever you come to me in the guise of suffering, it will be the most beautiful moment of my life. Your arrival shall be my feast!"

That same day someone who was feeling discouraged because of the difficulty of carrying out an apostolate in that large city came to see her. After listening to her, Chiara Lubich said,

> This morning I received Holy Communion and I told Jesus that I wanted to love him. Look, I've said this to him so many times before, but this morning it had a different flavor. The crucified will be my everything in life, and nothing else will matter to me. Before, I put up with suffering, even welcomed it, but I didn't see it as the best part of my Christian life, my highest aspiration, what I *should* cherish. Today I had the strength to do it and now throughout the day I search beneath the appearances of things, events or even people — for his face. He is my feast![23]

From then on Chiara's motto would be *Celebrate*! Celebrate Jesus forsaken and Paris will remain for you as "the city of festivity."[24] Here again, an endless desire to love him

---

23. Ibid., 217–218.
24. Chiara Lubich, *Diary 1964–1965* (Hyde Park, NY: New City Press, 1987), 110.

triggered a new and deeper love in Chiara, a love not merely endured but desired, filled with joy and open to new understanding of the mystery.

d) The many countenances of Jesus Forsaken (June 1972)

In October 1971 Chiara proposed to the members of the Focolare Movement that they meditate on and live out Jesus forsaken. She elaborated upon this reflection in seven talks, some of which were included in *The Cry* (2000). In June 1972 the focolarini gathered at the Movement's headquarters with Chiara to take stock of the year spent with Jesus forsaken. She gave a famous talk known as "The Countenances of Jesus Forsaken," in which she explained that she had learned to recognize her spouse, Jesus forsaken, clothed according to the circumstances in various guises—impossibility, doubt, blunder, brokenness…. Then, upon recognizing him she would smile at him and love him. When Michelangelo's *Pieta* was defaced, for example, she saw him as brokenness. Chiara described how she sought him out everywhere: he's here, he's there, he's everywhere. She said: "He peeps out everywhere." By loving him she discovered his loving presence everywhere.

e) If you don't love me, who will? (1980)

In 1980 the Focolare Movement was reflecting on the topic of God's will, well aware that "the will of God is our sanctification" (see 1 Thes 4:3). In November of that year Chiara once again asked for Jesus' help in deciding to become holy. One day she seemed to have found her answer in prayer. She thought and said to herself: "I have only one path for becoming holy. The will of God is only one thing for me: Jesus forsaken. Finish your life as you began it! Try to finish it with Jesus forsaken."[25] Having renewed this choice, within herself she again heard Jesus explaining the full scope of her decision, how he willed to use her to reveal himself in his forsakenness. Later, confiding this intimate experience to those close to her, she explained:

> And then during those days Jesus made me understand: "But if you don't love me, who will love me?" In the sense, "Look, after all these centuries, after twenty centuries, it is to you that I have revealed myself as the Forsaken One; it's as if I've uncovered this just for you. Then you spoke of it to many. But if you betray me, if you aren't my spouse, if you don't choose me alone as the will of God, leaving even the virtues behind, if you don't love me, who will love me? But do you realize that for twenty centuries I was always looking for you?"[26]

Through this experience Chiara understood the full extent of her call to love the forsaken One within the context of God's plan down through the ages.

There are two components therefore — light and love — and they are intrinsically linked. From the light flows more love, and from more love flows more light. They keep Chiara and those who follow her walking along the way of love for Jesus forsaken. She moves forward, enriching her life with new light and new love in the delicate balance and harmony between these two elements. Moreover, her life becomes theology: a return to the valley after a period of

---

25. As cited in Various Authors, *In profondita nell'unione con Dio*, (Rome: 2006), 67. Published for the use of the internal members of the Focolare Movement.
26. Ibid., 68.

contemplation, an illness, a large anonymous metropolis, the defaced Madonna of Michelangelo, a fervent longing for holiness...And many other such examples could be given in which she is drawn back to him, to her first love, where only in him does she find life.

It must be noted that what has been said so far concerning the centrality of love for Jesus forsaken in the life of Chiara Lubich and of those who follow her should not be misinterpreted to mean being empty in the face of suffering or loving suffering. It does not mean that you love suffering. It can never be stated enough that suffering—whether that of Jesus or of us—in itself is never redeeming. It is love that is redeeming. Jesus is the object of our love! Chiara states clearly that what is to be loved is not suffering, but only Jesus in the suffering.[27] At times, for the sake of simplicity she spoke of "loving the suffering," but those who follow her way understand her meaning; it is obvious that she means to love him. We will discuss God's mysterious presence in suffering later, but for now we can at least say that it derives from love, for it was out of love for us that Jesus took on our suffering (see Is 53:4–5) and out of love for us that God made him to be curse, sin (see Gal 3:13; 2 Cor 5:21). Suffering can become a point of encounter with him, a place of encounter between us and the One who has loved us. Jesus forsaken has taken on suffering, and in this gesture of love we love and recognize him. All of this takes place under the heading of love.

---

27. See Lubich, *Perche mi hai abandonato?*, D. Tratta, ed.(Rome: Città Nuova, 1997),16.

f) The trial of the final years (2004–2008)

In September 2004 Chiara entered into a deep spiritual trial, a dark night that seems to have lasted almost to the end of her life. Perhaps Jesus could not prevent his bride, the one to whom he had chosen to reveal his forsakenness, from reliving his own experience of it. As early as 1950, Chiara had gone through an abysmal dark night. In 1972 she alludes to it with an indirect reference to herself while speaking of the suffering of Mary at the foot of the cross:

> I think those who have received a special mission or calling from God can comprehend something of Mary's mysterious suffering. God often tests these people with a spiritual dark night, when they feel as if they have lost the light he had granted them, as to a prophet, for the good of his people. When this happens, these people, although they had been consistently aware of their calling, suffer indescribably and cry out at such abandonment.[28]

The trial that lasted from 2004 until 2008 was a very particular one, however, as one of Chiara's closest collaborators, Eli Folonari, attests:

> She no longer felt God. He didn't act. He didn't make himself felt. Chiara used the image of the sun disappearing over the horizon, disappearing, gone forever. We deduced from the written notes she left that this was the worst and most terrible night. She asked: Why am I alive? What am I doing on earth? What have I lived for if my Ideal no longer exists?[29]

---

28. Lubich, *Mary The Transparency of God*, 43.
29. *Città Nuova*, special edition (April 2008), 32.

We may never know any more than this; nevertheless, at least we do know that in this ultimate conformation to the Bridegroom Chiara discovered her theological personality as well as her mission in the Church. A few months before her death she said, "I suffer for all the sins of the world, for all the sinners."[30] Herein lies the complete fulfillment of Chiara's personality. Hans Urs von Balthasar says: "You do not become a person in any other way than by becoming with all the elect called to this vocation, brothers [and sisters] of the Firstborn."[31] Although Chiara never met von Balthasar personally she always held him in high regard. For him, "dying with the feeling of being abandoned by God is perhaps the highest form of union with the Lord."[32]

We now turn to the teaching method Chiara used in instructing her followers how to love Jesus forsaken.

---

30. Ibid.
31. Hans Urs von Balthasar, *La dramatique divine*, II: 27, *Culture et verite* (Namur: Lessius, 1988), 199. See also Rm 8:29.
32. He made this statement in reference to St. Thérèse of the Child Jesus, in *La priere contemplative* (Paris: Fayard, 1971), 260.

Chapter 2

THE DYNAMIC OF LOVING JESUS FORSAKEN

As soon as she discovered Jesus forsaken in that famous January of 1944, she did not keep her choice to love him to herself but communicated it to everyone in the vibrant community coming to life around her. Indeed, it was this choice that made the community so vibrant. She coined the expression, *Love (embrace) Jesus forsaken*. There is no doubt that for Chiara love for Jesus forsaken "summed up the whole of Christian life."[33] And she was most generous in her explanations as circumstances gradually led her to realize that Jesus forsaken should become *everything* in each person's life.

A singular and radical choice

Chiara said that the choice of Jesus forsaken was made in a "burst"[34] of love, a decision to suffer "with and like him,"[35] a vital decision: "a unique choice, a radical decision: Jesus forsaken."[36] Rereading the letters she had written in the early days of the Movement, she underscored the

---
33. See Anna Pelli, *L'abbandono di Gesu e il mistero del Dio uno e trino* (Rome: Città Nuova, 2000), 258–259.
34. Lubich, *The Cry*, 48.
35. Ibid.
36. Ibid., 61.

singular, radical, and absolute nature of this choice.[37] The repetition of certain words reveals the starkness of this choice: "none...but." "Therefore, we knew *none but* Him. We desired *none but* Christ and Him crucified." "Love for Him was exclusive and allowed for no compromise."[38] "Love of suffering that is synonymous with love of Jesus forsaken was like an obsession, as if everything would only be found there."[39]

Recognizing a presence of Christ in suffering means perceiving the meaning in reality

In *I have only one Spouse*, a document of primary importance for anyone who desires to love Jesus forsaken, Chiara states: "So it will be for the years I have left: athirst for suffering, anguish, despair, separation, exile, forsakenness, torment—for all that is him, and he is sin, hell."[40]

---

37. The letters of that time underscore this: "Forget everything...even the most sublime things. Allow yourself to be dominated by one only Idea, by one only God, who has to penetrate every fiber of your being: by Jesus forsaken" (July 21, 1945). "Do you know the lives of the saints? ...[It] was [all] summed up in a single word: Jesus crucified...the wounds of Christ were their resting place; the blood of Christ was the salutary bath for their souls; the wound in Christ's side was the coffin that they filled with their love. Ask Jesus, through his heartbreaking cry, for the passion of his passion. He must be everything for you"(July 21, 1945). "Jesus forsaken was the only book from which we wanted to read. 'Yes, it's true, I'm in university, but no book no matter how deep and beautiful, gives to my soul so much strength and, above all, so much love as Jesus crucified'"(June 7, 1944). Chiara Lubich, *Early Letters* (Hyde Park, NY: New City Press, 2012), 54–55.
38. Lubich, *The Cry*, 79.
39. Lubich, *Perche mi hai abbandonato?*, 59.
40. Lubich, The Cry, 61.

Several hundred times Chiara says that suffering is a face of Jesus forsaken: "Every single painful situation was a face of Jesus forsaken, darkness and boredom and cold and aridity and desperation and detachment and anguish and hunger and sorrow …with these things that impersonated Him."[41] Each of these was a "reflection" of Jesus forsaken, it was Jesus forsaken. "Suffering," she says, "is Jesus forsaken." "Behind the suffering there is his face."[42] But this quasi-identity has to be recognized continually, comprehended anew. You need to have the eyes for "seeing him," you need to try to discover him. Therefore this presence is both veiled and revealed. He reveals himself when you love him. Then you see him everywhere: "He fascinated us. Maybe we fell in love with Him because, right from the start, we had begun to see Him all over the place. He presented Himself with many different faces in all the sorrowful sides of life. They were nothing other than Him, only Him. Even though they were always new and different, they were always and simply Him."[43] Anna Pelli claims that Chiara could see "the likeness of Christ forsaken in the features of humanity."[44] Loving Jesus forsaken by choosing to love him in suffering because it is a revelation of true love, also means moving beyond the choice of loving him to understand reality and discover the presence of Christ within it.

---

41. Igino Giordani, *Erano I tempi di guerra: Agli albori dell'ideale dell'unita* (Rome: Città Nuova, 2007), 31.
42. Fabio Ciardi, *Cristo dispiegato nei secoli* (Rome: Città Nuova, 1994), 98.
43. Lubich, *The Cry*, 46.
44. Pelli, *L'abbandono di Gesu e il mistero del Dio uno e trino*, 257.

From embracing him to being consumed in one with him *(from acceptance to consummation)*

Chiara suggests that we love him in the suffering we encounter. Love him not because you "feel like it" but because "you want to." And she accompanies the word "love" with other words that are part of the logic of radicalism and exclusive decisions mentioned earlier: wanting him and therefore preferring him[45]; seeking him; celebrating him when he arrives.

Chiara's words convey the full scope of this dynamic: "Jesus forsaken, embraced, locked to one's self, wanted as our only all, he consumed in one with us, we consumed in one with him, made suffering with him Suffering: here lies everything."[46] Our love must come to be consumed in one with him, building gradually to a crescendo. When you embrace you are still two; by squeezing tight, the distance is reduced. But there is still space in this embrace for a refusal. And so the distance must be annihilated from within the person's deepest core, in his or her will, a will that must occupy all the space because it is a matter of wanting him, as Chiara has said, "as your exclusive all, saying that no other choice will ever satisfy us until we are consumed in Him, for He was consumed with us to the point of being one."

---

45. Lubich, "Mesaggio al Congresso internazionale del Movimento Umanità Nuova," Rimini, April 18–20 1997, in *Love Heals, a collection of thoughts and reflections of Chiara Lubich* (privately printed, January 2000), 85.
46. Lubich, *Essential Writings*, 96.

Reliving Jesus Forsaken by imitating his love creates a community of believers

If it stops at the suffering, love for Jesus forsaken is not authentic. Loving him means turning to others, going beyond ourselves, building up a community, the Church, the Body of Christ. Chiara often made this clear. She warned against the danger of remaining blocked in the suffering, in the pain.

What matters is love—she never tires of repeating—love for our neighbors. "But then you taught me to love you in my neighbor and when suffering came, I did not stop there but accepted it and, forgetful of myself, turned my thoughts to you standing at my side....So it was for years and years: the constant discipline of the cross, the asceticism of love. I underwent many trials and you know all about them, because you have counted the hairs on my head and numbered each one."[47] Another time she exhorted those who followed her: "We ...have our own way of loving our neighbor, a way that is all ours ...We love our neighbors to the point of reaching unity with them. We must love by loving one another. We must love in unity, and so we must have Jesus in our midst."[48] Jesus forsaken is the model, the way and the style of that love summarized in the words "make yourself one" with others as Jesus made himself one with us. Moreover, Jesus forsaken ensures the fruitfulness of the soil.

> We should put ourselves on the level of others to make ourselves one, to make unity with them. Just as the Word became one with us and made us God's children by becoming incarnate, so should

---

47. Ibid., 56–57.
48. Lubich, *Il cammino col Risorto*, 102.

> we learn to 'descend' with everyone in order to then ascend with them. This would seem to be an abasement, a diminishing; actually, it's an increasing in love.... This is why we have to be empty, because we have to be like Jesus forsaken who is our model.[49]

Then Jesus is the *Way*: "Yes, this is the way because it is the same path which was followed by God in order to manifest his love. He became a person like us, crucified and abandoned in order to place Himself at the same level as everyone else; truly weak with those who are weak."[50]

Jesus forsaken teaches this art of making yourself one, this art of loving. In some notes from the early days of the Movement she writes: "We ought to be one with our neighbor, not in an idealized way, but in a real way. Not in a future way but in the present. Being one means feeling in ourselves what our neighbors feel. Dealing with their feelings as if they were our own, making them our own through our concern. Being them, doing this for the love of Jesus in our neighbor. To be able to love our neighbors, we've got to transform this cold and stony heart of ours into a heart of flesh."[51]

> Jesus forsaken is our style of love. He teaches us to empty ourselves of everything inside us and around us, to "make ourselves one" with God; he teaches us to put aside our thoughts and attach-

---

49. Various authors, *Come un arcobaleno. Gli "aspetti" del movimento dei Focolari*, for internal use by the Focolare Movement (Rome: 1999), 120–121.
50. Chiara Lubich, *La vita un viaggio* (Rome: Città Nuova, 1985), 32–33. In the same source, see 82, "Let us love one another as He has loved us. Jesus loved us to the abandonment. Let us love each brother or sister in this way."
51. Lubich, *Unity and Jesus Forsaken*, 29.

ments, to mortify our senses, to drop even our own inspirations so that we can "make ourselves one" with our neighbors, which means to serve them, to love them. The radicalness that characterized our first choice of Jesus forsaken, the decision to see nothing else, strikes us even today as a message, a specific and urgent invitation to renew our choice of him as the only love of our life. It comes to us like a warning not only to embrace and see in all our pains a meeting with a beloved Spouse, expected and consequently welcomed "always, immediately, and joyfully" but to look at him as the gauge of our love of neighbor: a measureless measure in our duty to give our all, reserving nothing for ourselves, not even what seem to be the most spiritual values, even the most divine; to imitate his manner of loving, even to the heroic practice of all the virtues included in love.[52]

In practicing the art of "making yourself one" you find the "cross on which to nail yourself,"[53] which is also a source of life for us and for others. In fact, if this love becomes "mutual, it is Life itself come among us. It is Jesus."[54]

It is life and growth of the Christian community. We reach "that marvelous result which the apostle Paul aspired to: being all things to all people; making himself one with everyone in order to win the greatest number to Christ (see 1 Cor 9:19). If we made ourselves one with our neighbors,

---

52. Ibid., 51.
53. Ibid., 31.
54. Ibid.

we could pass our Ideal on to them."[55] In another place she says that this love will bring a miraculous catch.[56]

Even though Chiara's words are more than clear, it is important to reiterate that Jesus forsaken correctly understood, that is, as the culmination of the dynamic of love of the Father in giving the Son to us and of the Son giving himself to the Father for us in fulfillment of the Incarnation, also leads us to love our neighbors. Our "making ourselves the other" is the image of God's "making Himself one." Therefore, far from being a devotional practice, love for Jesus forsaken is a participation in the very life of God, loving as God loves.

Love for Jesus Forsaken is the experience of the triumphant entry of God into the soul, an Easter event

The effects of love for Jesus forsaken are related not to intellectual knowledge but to lived experience. They are the verifications through experience of the central truth of the faith: This man you crucified and killed, God has raised up (see Acts 2:23–24). What you experience is the triumphal entry of God into the soul in an anticipated Easter.

Take the example of one young man injured at age nineteen in a motorcycle accident, who spent the next thirty-five years in a wheelchair. He accepted his condition as one of the faces of Jesus forsaken. He studied medicine and became an expert in robot technology. Now he gives conferences, advises architects, makes connections with people all over the world. In our telephone conversations and personal encounters he has said, over and over, that this accident was the greatest grace of his life. It allowed

---

55. Chiara Lubich, *La vita un viaggio*, 16–17.
56. Ibid., 89.

Chapter 2 The Dynamic Of Loving Jesus Forsaken

him to encounter Jesus forsaken. Another example is a priest who works with street children in Brazil. He said that at first he never understood why Chiara Lubich chose Jesus forsaken as her Spouse. He wondered how you could fall in love with such an ugly and disfigured spouse. Then he understood, little by little, that Jesus forsaken is the God Man who gives his life in loving to the end without expecting anything in return.

And so love for Jesus forsaken produces a flow of light and revelation. From that moment back in 1944 when the priest first revealed to Chiara the love of God in Jesus forsaken, a river of wisdom began to flow, a torrent that became the heritage of the Focolare Movement, born solely from Jesus forsaken.

In the final analysis, loving Jesus forsaken is an encounter with the risen Lord. You discover that "beneath it all [the suffering] it was him, the only true God, perfect Peace, fullness of Joy, Light…all the things that are not of this world."[57] The face is that of Jesus forsaken, yes, but Jesus is God. With amazement Chiara Lubich exclaims, "We have chosen you on the cross, in your most forsaken state, to be our all, and you have then given us paradise on earth. You are God, God, God."[58]

This is the experience of a divine alchemy by which "a suffering that has been loved as a face of Jesus crucified and forsaken can transform into joy,"[59] be medicine[60] and true life.[61] All the writings from the early times refer to this experience of having loved Jesus forsaken and then finding God. It is a sharing in the Redemption as described in the

---

57. Giordani, *Erano tempi di Guerra*, 31.
58. Lubich, *Jesus: The Heart of His Message*, 35.
59. Lubich, *In cammino col Risorto*, 171.
60. See *The Cry*, 53.
61. Ibid., 54.

text *I have only one Spouse*: "I will dry up the waters of tribulation in many hearts nearby and, through communion with my almighty Spouse, in many far away."[62] It is a sharing in Divine Life: "Here is how we become (by participation) God, Love."[63]

Among the many texts that illustrate this Resurrection experience, one from the 1950's is particularly significant. *Remember, Jesus?*[64] is written in the form of a prayer:

> Remember, Jesus, when I was young, I asked You to …"Give me the passion of Your Passion!"? How impenetrable Your Suffering was! And how inaccessible it seemed to me! But You heard my desire, which You yourself had placed within me, and you heard the prayer and then began your work, making me taste something of Your own sufferings.
>
> First I realized that a hidden Wound existed in Your Heart, hidden, unknown, undiscovered and totally spiritual. Compared to it, the Wound in Your Side even seemed such a small thing to me. This was the wound of the Abandonment—that terrible Trauma of Your soul.

In this passage, Chiara reveals what, after nineteen centuries of Christian history, is completely new in the revelation of Jesus forsaken. This wound was left hidden, unknown and undiscovered. She is aware that Jesus has given her a highly uncommon gift, which came with the responsibility of making this suffering known. The text continues:

---

62. Lubich, *Essential Writings*, 95.
63. Ibid., 96.
64. It is quoted almost in its entirety in "L'unione con Dio," *Nuova Umanità* Vol. 153–154(Rome, 2004), 335.

> Then, little by little, you made me enter into Your suffering, Your infinite Pain!
>
> And, then, something never before heard of: beyond the doorway that spoke to me of infinite anguish and death, I found Love and the suffering vanished.
>
> I've discovered the law of Life.
>
> Jesus, You know what I'm saying.
>
> Whoever enters into Your infinite pain finds, as if by magic, that everything is transformed into Love. It's God beneath that veil of infinite anguish and, in Him, the created Universe and the uncreated Heaven. I've found the secret treasure, all knowledge, every good thing, every love, every beauty. I've found the Life.

She repeats that he is present beneath the countless nuances of suffering: "You made me enter into Your suffering: Your infinite Suffering!" Commenting on this text in October 2003, she added: "I've seen him under a thousand guises and loved him as is." Then she bursts into a song of wonder at what she discovers there, expressing her awe as she discovers that suffering is actually the door that opens onto the Life of God. She even goes so far as to say that suffering which is loved leads to an encounter with God. Seldom was she ever so explicit: By loving Jesus forsaken you discover "the law of Life, all knowledge, all beauty, all love." This is a new awareness that springs from a life in union with Jesus forsaken. In the infinite suffering of Jesus "God is [present] beneath that veil of infinite anguish." Armed with this discovery, she has good reason to ask: What about Your suffering, Lord? Where is the suffering? The text continues:

Jesus, beautiful Jesus, where is Your great Suffering? I knew that it was all Love. But that it was actually like this? I would never have imagined!... Who will ever understand me? Jesus, You understand me because I am in You and You are in me. And those who are with me are in You.

She concludes with a stupendous prayer in which she asks for his very own love, so that she can love him in perfect reciprocity: "Grant me to love You as You love me."

Through love for Jesus Forsaken the risen Lord radiates the gifts of the Holy Spirit

In the focolare spirituality, the Holy Spirit's role in love for Jesus forsaken is not usually highlighted.[65] This reality is consciously lived, but only after time has passed can such experiences be reflected upon. When this does happen, it is a joyous discovery. In the 1980s, when with the help of theologians Chiara was reflecting on Jesus forsaken, she discovered the relationship between Jesus forsaken and the gift of the Spirit to the Church.[66]

---

65. It is mentioned only a few times in the writings from the early times: "We have to have the nothingness of Jesus forsaken, which is infinite nothingness. The Holy Spirit will then rest within us. Love must be distilled to the point of being only the Holy Spirit. It is distilled when it passes through Jesus forsaken." Lubich, *Essential Writings*, 148.
66. Chiara reflects on the relationship between the Spirit and Jesus forsaken in *Jesus: The Heart of His Message*, 75. For example, regarding the gospel verse: "Then Jesus bowed his head and gave up his spirit" (Jn 19:30), Chiara cites Stanislaus Lyonnet: "John's expression, with reference to the death of Jesus, `he bowed his head, and delivered over his spirit' is unusual. The verb `delivered over' [his spirit] seems to have been chosen to indicate Christ's voluntary offering of his life. Using a very unusual expression to refer to Jesus'

Here she returns again to her lived experience affirming that in the early times "Jesus forsaken, …once loved, filled us with [the] Holy Spirit, because precisely there on the cross when his side was torn open, blood and water immediately flowed out, and [the] Holy Spirit," and "anyone who loved Jesus forsaken gains [the] Holy Spirit."[67] Therefore, she explains, there is a logical connection between embracing the abandoned Lord and experiencing the fullness of freedom, love and Holy Spirit.[68] She cites John Paul II's address to diocesan priests of the Focolare Movement on April 30, 1982: "Embracing the suffering Jesus in our daily trials immediately unites us with the Spirit of the Risen One and his strengthening power" (see Rom 6:5; Phil 1:19).[69]

Every gift of the Spirit blossoms in us when there is love for Jesus forsaken: patience, perseverance, meekness, peace, but above all the Holy Spirit's excellent gift—love. It is the Spirit who loves in us, expressing love with all the nuances of mercy:

When we have known suffering in all shades of its most frightful forms, in the most varied kinds of anguish, and have stretched out our arms to God in mute, heart-rending supplication, uttering subdued cries for help; when we have

---

death, John meant to tell us that the effect of his death was the gift of the Spirit to the community." See also Marisa Cerini, *God who is Love in the experience and thought of Chiara Lubich*, (Hyde Park, NY: New City Press, 1992) 80, note 20.
67. Chiara Lubich, *L'amore risana*, (Rome: Jan. 2000), 48. Published for the use of the internal members of the Focolare Movement.
68. "Therefore it is not a contradiction, but in accordance with the Passion of Jesus and the mystery of salvation.… Embracing the Cross well, all the way, and then throwing yourself into loving, makes the Holy Spirit come into your heart, explode in your heart. And so there's no contradiction there." *Chiara Lubich responde ai volontari 1960–2012*, privately printed (Rome: 2003), 221.
69. Lubich, *The Cry*, 121.

drunk the chalice to the last drop and have offered to God, for days and years, our own cross mingled with his, which gives it divine value, then God has pity on us and welcomes us into union with him.

This is the moment in which, having experienced the unique value of suffering, having believed in the economy of the cross and seen its beneficial effects, God shows us in a new and higher way something that is worth even more than suffering. It is love for others in the form of mercy, the love that stretches our hearts and arms to embrace the wretched, the poor, those whom life has ravaged, repentant sinners.[70]

Loving and reliving Jesus forsaken communicates God's love to us.

As the source of happiness, Jesus Forsaken asks that we love him with pure love

In the final analysis, love for Jesus forsaken brings happiness. It is neither attachment to sorrow nor to pain, because it is always a response to a divine revelation. Chiara confirms: "You don't love the suffering which is always something negative, but Jesus in the suffering"[71]

But he asks for pure love, that we be glad to be with him in suffering,[72] to communicate with him, to drink the chalice to the dregs, to have no pretenses. Love for Jesus is Chiara's only motivation, love that longs to consume itself with the beloved. "Jesus needs souls able to love him to the point of choosing him not for the joy of following him, not for paradise and the eternal reward he is preparing for

---

70. Lubich, *Essential Writings*, 85.
71. Lubich, *Perche mi hai abbandonato?*, 140.
72. Ibid.

us, not just to 'feel good.' No. But only because the soul thirsting for true love wants to be consumed with His."[73]

It is a love that, out of love for him, strives to emulate his love. [74]

Experiencing that God in Christ allows us to share in his riches, making himself known to us when we share in his sufferings, prompts us to love Jesus forsaken solely for himself, not only because of the joy of the resurrection—at least while we are still on this earth. For this reason, on several occasions Chiara warned that we do not love Jesus forsaken in order to rise out of suffering, but only to love him for himself. Thus, in a casual conversation, she once remarked,

> At first Jesus presents Himself as your Spouse, giving you the joy of communion with him. Now he presents Himself to you again, but forsaken so that you can embrace him. Therefore, you should say: "I'm truly happy, because I don't live to have a relationship with you, but to love you." I assure you that if you really and truly embrace him and never try to manipulate him or exploit him for the joy of being with him—this is where you can go wrong—if you love him for Himself, then he alone will give you the fullness of joy and you will once again feel united to him.[75]

Loving Jesus Forsaken is a mission

The experience of loving Jesus forsaken cannot be kept hidden quietly. You feel sent out to proclaim it. This mission is explained well in the foundational document *I have*

---

73. Lubich, *The Cry*, 41.
74. Ibid., 37.
75. Lubich, *Perche mi hai abandonato?*, 110–111.

only one Spouse. It is a mission accomplished within space and time: "I will go through the world seeking…" opening heart and mind to suffering humankind, to refugees, to those who suffer because of war, to underdevelopment, to divisions in the world,[76] to anybody who is alone, seeing in them the face of Jesus forsaken.

It is a mission accomplished in time: "So it will be for the years I have left: athirst for suffering, anguish, despair" in order to lift people out of their slavery of suffering. "*I will dry up* the waters of tribulation in many hearts nearby and, through communion with my almighty Spouse, in many far away" and pass "as a fire that consumes all that must fall and *leaves standing only* the truth," which is a share in the good news that suffering and death have been conquered, freeing the energy contained in the abandoned-risen Lord and perceiving the true meaning of reality.

Mary Desolate, icon of the one who loves Jesus Forsaken[77]

For Chiara, Mary is the icon of the one who loves Jesus forsaken and generates the New Creation. In her desolation Mary reaches the apex of her design, just as in the abandonment Jesus reaches the culmination of his love for the Father and for us:

---

76. "You will find him in the sick: he was seriously ailing and dying. You will find him in the prisoners: he was nailed down. You will find him in all the ones you are planning to visit in your cities. You can see him in them all! He is the strongest reason why you feel urged to carry on with Operation Africa, another aspect of your revolution. Jesus forsaken is a perfect snapshot of the abandoned African people, sick, lost and so poor, a people heading for extinction." *Ai Gen 3* (Rome: Città Nuova, 1979), 34.
77. "To be Mary, you need to be Jesus forsaken," in Lubich, *Mary Transparency of God*, 97.

We saw furthermore how the riches that Jesus bore in Himself were fully displayed when he was crucified. His abandonment completely revealed his nature as Savior. Jesus, in his forsakenness, gave Himself totally. Like Jesus, Mary also had her moment of culmination. It was her desolation, which is her forsakenness.[78]

Mary in her desolation is the one who teaches how to love Jesus forsaken. As mentioned earlier, you become another Mary by going beyond the wound. If you follow and imitate her in her desolation, you are re-clothed with her unique prerogatives, for the good of the Church and the world. Chiara explains:

> Loving Jesus forsaken ensures that the words of St. Paul are true for us: "For I decided to know nothing among you except Jesus Christ, and him crucified" (1 Cor 2:2). Don't give importance to anything but Jesus forsaken in the suffering, Jesus forsaken in the detachments, Jesus forsaken in the effort to live the virtues, particularly love toward your brothers and sisters, and especially toward enemies and those who resemble Jesus forsaken. With Him we will be like Mary. We will be strong, loving, pure, amiable, lovable, prudent, powerful, wise, merciful, faithful, and so on…. Love toward Jesus Forsaken, our spouse, will make us… mothers and fathers of many souls. Like Mary we will be "house of gold" because we will preserve the presence of the risen Lord in us which shines like gold. We will be "ark of the covenant" because we will never break the covenant we've made with Him, to love Him above all things. We will be "gate of heaven" for many who will be

---

78. Ibid., 38–39.

saved though our love. We will be "morning star" because like her we will shine in a dark world. We will be "health of the sick" because we will do all in our power to alleviate the pain of those who suffer. We will be "refuge and hope of sinners" because they will turn to us when their hearts are ready to open. We will be "consoler of the afflicted" because we will bring joy to hearts that are sickened and wounded. And we will be "help of Christians" because we will enter into loving dialogue....There is much about Mary that could be imitated by loving Jesus Forsaken. In fact, I would dare say that anyone who has even just decided to love Jesus forsaken already resembles Mary, at least in some of these ways.[79]

We conclude by observing how the many facets of love for Jesus forsaken in the life of Chiara Lubich encompass every characteristic of faith. In the parable of the sower (Lk 8:4–15) the seed of faith is "held fast in an honest and good heart" (v. 15) that seeks truth. Down through the years Chiara accepted that seed over and over, even when she was in danger of being overtaken by worries and concerns. Above all, the seed has borne "much fruit with patient endurance" (v. 15b) creating a new Work of God, the vineyard of Jesus forsaken.

For anyone who would follow this way, choosing and loving Jesus forsaken must never waver from being a response to God's love, a love revealed in the abandonment of Jesus and in every painful situation in life. It is this response that will reach all the way to sharing and participating in his

---

79. Cited in L.M. Salierno, *Maria negli scritti di Chiara Lubich*, (Rome: Città Nuova, 1993), 172–173..

suffering, so that we then may participate in his Resurrection and his mission of uniting people.

This is an authentic act of faith because it is, above all, a living acceptance of the mystery of the Incarnation of the Word in human history. You "believe" and adhere in a living way to the revelation that God took on human flesh, became one of us in all things, taking on our human condition entirely, even our separation from God and, in doing so, divinized it.

It is also a living adherence to the central tenet of the faith: the resurrection of Jesus, the event that stands at the core of Christian life. In fact, only someone who believes in the Resurrection is able to embrace death. In each embrace of death one is stating tacitly: "I believe that you have risen!" This is not in order to make the suffering disappear but in order to welcome with love the Christ who has loved and given himself for us. Therefore, it is neither love of suffering for the sake of suffering, nor a process for making the suffering disappear. It is not philosophy or psychology. It is faith and love for Christ who has been revealed and known in scripture and in the Church.

By loving and reliving Jesus forsaken we relive the Lord in his incarnation, passion, death and resurrection. The entire mystery of Jesus is contemplated in this act of love. Love for Jesus forsaken engages our entire being: our freedom, our reason and our will. This love is also characterized by an ever-deeper knowledge of the mystery. This mutual implication between faith and knowledge is described by the Catechism of the Catholic Church as "a more penetrating knowledge [which] will in turn call forth a greater faith, increasingly set afire by love" (no. 158). This process of faith through knowledge and knowledge through faith can be verified in the life of Chiara Lubich, who strove during her entire life to enter the mystery of Jesus forsaken through her love, through her faith.

We now move on to consider Chiara Lubich's insights regarding Jesus forsaken, insights that truly can be called "theological."

Chapter 3

Faith to Understanding and Understanding to Faith: Who is Jesus Forsaken?

An understanding of God has emerged from this way of Christian living, a reliable source of knowledge about who God is. It recalls the experience of Augustine: "I believe to better understand, and learn to better believe" (Sermon 43, 7, 9). He shines light on a *perichoresis* between faith and understanding, knowledge of that same faith.

It is particularly interesting to note that if for us Jesus forsaken is a word pronounced by God and welcomed in faith, source of the knowledge of who God is, communication of the reality of God and therefore at the same time salvation and divinization, as Chiara Lubich points out, he is also *in himself* the culmination of the revelation; that is, of the communication that God makes of himself, model of faith, source of the knowledge of love, realization of a new creation already underway.

Having made himself nothingness of love, he is the culmination of revelation

The incarnation is the summit of revelation. As John says: "No one has ever seen God. It is God the only Son, who is close to the Father's heart, who has made him known" (Jn 1:18). The cross and abandonment are the ultimate consequence of the incarnation. Chiara expresses it in a statement that builds to a crescendo: "He became man, then bread, then *nothing* in his abandonment."[80] The cross and abandonment are, therefore, the fullness of revelation, sources of revelation: "It is in the abandonment and in his death on the cross that Jesus fully shows Himself to be light of the Father, revealer of Trinitarian love, Wisdom unfolded and totally bestowed."[81]

Jesus forsaken, Chiara explains, is the Word of God incarnate and completely revealed[82] and therefore, as the Word, the fullness of God's presence.[83] "If we want to know who God is, then we must fall on our knees at the foot of the cross."[84]

By becoming a nothingness of love, Jesus Forsaken is the faith

While experiencing the loss of his relationship with God, Jesus lovingly re-abandons himself to the Father in an attitude that could be called an attitude of faith: "In fact nobody has had greater trust than he; forsaken by God, he trusted in God; forsaken by Love, he entrusted Himself to Love."[85] Piero Coda writes: "I would not hesitate to say that in the abandonment event Jesus lives out the maximum intensity of faith. Indeed, as Chiara Lubich says so succinctly: 'Jesus forsaken is the faith' because he re-abandons

---

80. See Lubich, *Incontri con l'Oriente*, 181.
81. *Come un arcobaleno*, 524.
82. "We have always admired Jesus crucified and forsaken as the Word completely unfolded." Lubich, *La vita un viaggio*, 88.
83. Lubich, *Essential Writings*, 120.
84. Juergen Moltmann, cited in Bruno Forte, *Piccola introduzione alla fede* (Alba: SocietàSan Paolo, 2005), 31.
85. Lubich, *The Cry*, 56.

Himself to the Father in the very moment when he feels abandoned by the Father."[86]

It is interesting to note that in recent texts Chiara has said that in his forsakenness Jesus is, at the same time, the image of one who re-abandons to the Father. More and more often she has spoken of him in relation to [that declaration of loving abandon] "Father, into your hands..." (Lk 23:46); as the one who while feeling abandoned by love, re-abandons himself to love. She also often began adding the adjective "risen" to the word "forsaken": "The forsaken and risen Lord."[87]

His nothingness provides some understanding of trinitarian love

Jesus is the Word completely revealed. In his abandonment he expresses God's love for us by reaching out to us in our distance from God. He breaks into our history of sin and exile and allows us to know God and share in his life. But also in and of himself, Jesus forsaken reveals that God is love. The Father is actively involved in the work of Redemption as the one who "did not spare his own Son" (Rom 8:32), who "so loved the world that he gave his only Son" (Jn 3:16). Trinitarian love is revealed on the Son's cross. Through his death in obedience to the Father, Jesus reveals that love is simultaneously death and life[88] or, in Chiara's terms, "Love is and is not at the same time."[89] Precisely in his emptiness, as he loses God, he reveals God for who

---

86. Piero Coda, *La fede: un'introduzione*, in *La Fede, evento e promessa*, Piero Coda and Christian Hennecke, eds. (Rome: Città Nuova, 2000), 22.
87. Lubich, *The Cry*, 137.
88. See François Varillon, *Gioia di credere, gioia di vivere* (Bologna: Edizioni Dehoniane, 1989).
89. Giuseppe Maria Zanghí, "Alcuni cenni su Gesu Abbandonato," *Nuova Umanità* (1998/3–4), 407.

God is and not what human beings would like God to be.[90] Only those who understand love understand the cross as the revelation and explanation of love.[91] Chiara would one day call Jesus forsaken the revelation of the "super-love."[92]

Because he becomes nothing out of love, he receives the gift of the resurrection, the fullness of unity

In his very death, Jesus rises. In fact, the redemption brought about by Jesus is a gift of love to the Father,[93] gift of his body but also of his soul as he is stripped of his equality

---

90. See Varillon, 75–76. The Son obeys the Father in order to "reveal him in his true being and not as men would want him to be. For Jesus, revealing God in this way, as he is, meant accepting death. If Jesus had not accepted death, he would not have revealed God as he is. In fact, the real substance of things is that in God, death is forever in the very heart of life. God is Love. Now, love means dying to yourself; not only preferring others over yourself…but renouncing to exist for yourself and through yourself in order to exist only through others and for others…. Living is loving, but loving is dying because it means existing only through others and for others."
91. "But what is not understood is love par excellence: which is to understand that God who made us, came on earth as one human being among others, lived with us, and allowed himself to be nailed to a cross: to save us.
    It is too high, too beautiful, too divine, too little human, too bloodstained, painful, intense to be understood." Lubich, *Essential Writings*, 90.
    "In short, the cross is the necessary instrument by which the divine penetrates the human, and a human being participates more fully in the life of God." Lubich, *Essential Writings*, 91.
92. Chiara spoke about this revelation of a super-love in a talk at the Cathedral of Aachen, Germany, on November 13, 1998. It refers to a term used by a Buddhist monk who, through the Focolare Movement, had discovered that the Crucifix was the "super-love."
93. "It is the end point of Jesus' self-giving." Pelli, *L'abbandono di Gesù e il mistero del Dio uno e trino*, 260.

with God. Because of this gift of Jesus to the Father, the Father raises him up. Jesus re-abandons himself to the Father so that the Father may raise him up. By re-abandoning himself to the Father who abandons him, Jesus consents to being generated as the Son in his humanity as well. If in the abandonment Jesus reaches full unity with the Father as a man; in the resurrection the Father responds and glorifies the man-Jesus, establishing him in "glorious power and truth as the Son."[94] As Chiara loved to say, he is the key, the secret to unity with God and with one another.

In the passages from the illuminative period during 1949, Chiara observes the continuity between death and life, even the contemporaneity. "But having emptied Himself out of love, to the point of becoming sin, absolute nothingness, hell—Jesus rediscovers Himself to be the Holy One, Absolute Fullness, Heaven."[95] He gave God and rediscovered God in Himself [in his humanity] and in everyone."[96] "In becoming nothing, Jesus still remains Absolute Fullness because he is Fully Love, [the] Absolute Being, Pure Love. Not the Absolute Being clothed by Love."[97] Jesus rises already in his abandonment. "By becoming sin, he became Nothingness. In him Nothingness is so united to Absolute Fullness (God) that whatever belongs to one belongs to the other. And so Nothingness becomes Fullness: Jesus Forsaken is God. Jesus-sin is God; Jesus-Nothingness is God; Jesus-Hell is God."[98]

---

94. Durrwell, *Christ notre paque*, 30.
95. In Blaumeiser, *Un mediatore che è nulla*, 405.
96. In Zanghi, *Alcuni cenni su Gesu Abbandonato*, 36.
97. Ibid.
98. In Blaumeiser, *Un mediatore che è nulla*, 398.

Because he is nothing, he is the new creation

With the marks of his suffering and ours the living Christ has radically changed the course of history. Because he assumed everything there was in us—even death, even being abandoned by God and re-abandoning himself to God who raised him up from his death—he is present in everything that smacks of abandonment, suffering, or death. He has entered into every fiber of creation—every living being and every situation. He is there behind every suffering, and his resurrection from the dead is living and active in that suffering as well.

Chiara expresses this in her mystical writings from 1949:

> The Father sent the Son on earth to mix in with created things, to recapitulate and divinize them. Jesus the Mediator was the cause of the marriage between the Uncreated and the created, of the unity between the created and Uncreated …with the end result that everything was God: God in Himself and God in creation.[99]

"Jesus forsaken breathed in all the vanity and the vanity became him and He is God. There is no longer emptiness on earth, nor in Heaven: there's God."[100] "But Jesus, having annihilated Himself out of love for the Father and for us, having annihilated Himself even so far as to make Himself sin, absolute nothing, hell, He found Himself Holy, All, God, Paradise, and with Him makes Holy, All, God, Paradise, his brothers and sisters for whom he suffered and died."[101] Moreover, says Chiara, God sees all things

---

99. Ibid., 393.
100. Ibid., 397.
101. Ibid., 405.

through Jesus forsaken, who is the pupil of his eye: "The Father, and whoever is in the bosom of the Father, sees Jesus forsaken everywhere; that is, he sees Himself: God. And so everywhere he sees God: Paradise."[102] Therefore she can summarize splendidly: "suffering is now love."[103] We are already in the end times, already within salvation.

She expresses it particularly well in her address upon receiving an honorary degree in Mexico City on June 6, 1997:

> Jesus forsaken experienced in Himself and took upon Himself the nonbeing of all those separated from the source of being: he took upon Himself the "vanity of vanities" (Eccl 1:2).
>
> Out of love, he made his own this non-being that we can call negative and transformed it into Himself, into the positive non-being that is love, as revealed in the resurrection. Jesus forsaken made the Holy Spirit overflow into creation, thus becoming "mother" of the new creation.[104]

A new creation is at work at the heart of history, working from within and leaving its mark. Jesus forsaken became Absolute Fullness. Everything is divinized. Anything that bears the mark of Jesus forsaken simultaneously bears the mark of the risen Lord. Even Hell is Jesus forsaken: "Jesus Forsaken, who made Himself Nothing, gave existence also to this non-being, hence also to hell, to death. He made death become living.."[105] Chiara speaks of this when she recalls the experience of that illuminative period of 1949

---

102. Ibid., 398.
103. Lubich, *Essential Writings*, 95.
104. Ibid., 213.
105. In Hubertus Blaumeiser, "All'infinito verso la disunità," *Nuova Umanità* (1997/5) 569.

twelve years later: "It seemed to me that through Jesus forsaken the duality of the Afterlife was wiped out and that Jesus forsaken was the solution, the contact between the two realms where in one Eternal Life is lived and in the other Eternal Death.."[106]

Chiara's reflection, which emerged from a life spent loving him, highlights how making himself nothing makes Jesus forsaken the revelation of God *par excellence*, faith *par excellence*, Love *par excellence*, fullness of unity, the new creation already underway. Jesus forsaken, when examined with a mind illuminated by faith, communicates the reality of God, a model of faith, an explanation of the nature of both Trinitarian Love and love in itself, the source of life and salvation.

Conclusion

For Chiara Lubich, love for Jesus forsaken is a choice that involves the whole person in responding to a revelation. It leads to a deep participation in the resurrection of Jesus, to divinization. Everything begins with love for Jesus forsaken and for our brothers and sisters, and everything flows into love for Jesus forsaken and for our brothers and sisters.

Love for Jesus forsaken is therefore deep union with Christ. It echoes the marriage bond, but for the sake of building up the community. There is nothing in it of attachment to sorrow or private personal experience. It is sharing in the entire mystery of Jesus, not only from the incarnation to the passion, death, and resurrection, but also the ascension and Pentecost.

Now we shall proceed to examine similar concepts in the New Testament.

---

106. Lubich, "Paradise '49," 11–12.

Part 2

HOW HUMANKIND RELATES TO THE PASCHAL MYSTERY IN THE NEW TESTAMENT

After examining the rich and complex reality behind "love for Jesus forsaken," we now turn our attention to corresponding ideas in the New Testament. We will examine in particular how the New Testament presents someone who embraces the mystery of Christ and shares in the mystery of the abandonment.

Chapter 4

In Paul's writings

Revelation of the Paschal Mystery in Paul

The letters of Paul, who encountered the risen Lord on the road to Damascus, are filled with proclamations of what he had seen and experienced. The sole object of his faith and preaching is the one who had died for our sins, apparently cursed by God, whom God raised!

This revelation disrupts everything in his life. In God's name Saul of Tarsus had been fighting against someone whom God had raised! This changed all his parameters, the structure of his logic, his way of thinking. It would redefine his entire existence and place him on a new path of life as a preacher. I think that for Paul a way of thinking flowed from this, a paradigm that took different forms but was always structured in a way similar to the Beatitudes: whatever smacks of suffering is a source of life. This is the paradox when it comes to God: curse becomes blessing; death becomes life. Put negatively, the power of God is not what we think it is; the wisdom of God is not what we believe.[107] Put positively, on the Cross God revealed the

---

107. "The true God is different from what human beings think God is; God does not correspond to the human question about God...The true God is a surprise beyond human comparison for man. He is beyond all his representations and expectations." Georg Eichholz,

divine way of acting. God used what is not, in order to reduce to nothing what is (see 1 Cor 1:28), used scandal and folly to demonstrate divine wisdom and power.[108] Paul combines opposites to demonstrate that they now form and exist according to a new logic.

This way of thinking is at work first in the life of Christ where poverty generates wealth: "For you know the generous act of our Lord Jesus Christ, that though he was rich, yet for your sakes he became poor, so that by his poverty you might become rich" (2 Cor 8:9). The curse of one generates salvation for all: "For our sake he made him to be sin who knew no sin, so that in him we might become the righteousness of God" (2 Cor 5:21). Notice that both sentences are structured identically: he became what he *was not*, *for us*, to make us sharers of what *he is*. This same structure is found in the song to the Philippians: "Though he was in the form of God, [he] did not regard equality with God something to be grasped at, but he humbled himself and became obedient to the point of death—even death on a cross" (Phil 2:8). The death of one is life for everyone. We are possessed by the love of Christ, "because we are convinced that one has died for all; therefore all have died. And he died for all, so that those who live might live no longer for themselves, but for him who died and was raised for them." (2 Cor 5:14–15). In another place Paul writes:

Die Teologie des Paulus im Umriss (Neukirchen: Neukirchener Verlag, 1972), 59, in Gérard Rossé, "La fede in San Paolo" (Piero Coda and Christian Hennecke, eds. *La Fede, evento e promessa*, 146–147).

108. "For Jews demand signs and Greeks desire wisdom, but we proclaim Christ crucified, a stumbling block to Jews and foolishness to Gentiles, but to those who are the called, both Jews and Greeks, Christ the power of God and the wisdom of God. For God's foolishness is wiser than human wisdom, and God's weakness is stronger than human strength" (1 Cor 1:22–25).

"But where sin abounded, grace abounded even more" (Rm 5:20). We find these opposites composed in a new logic within the apostle's own life: what is a gain he considers a loss, with respect to the knowledge of Christ's resurrection (see Phil 3:8). Nothing can shake his hope:

> We are afflicted in every way, but not crushed; perplexed, but not driven to despair; persecuted, but not forsaken; struck down, but not destroyed; always carrying in the body the death of Jesus, so that the life of Jesus may also be made visible in our bodies. For while we live, we are always being given up to death for Jesus' sake, so that the life of Jesus may be made visible in our mortal flesh. (2 Cor 4:8–11)

Tribulations are never void of consolation. On the contrary, where sufferings of Christ abound, consolation also abounds: "He consoles us in all our affliction" (2 Cor 1:4a).

The same logic plays out in the relationships between the apostle and the members of the churches that Paul established. If he is consoled in his affliction, it is only so that he can console those that are in danger: "so that we may be able to console those who are in any affliction with the consolation with which we ourselves are consoled by God" (2 Cor 1:4b). When revealing to the Corinthians the sufferings he has had to endure, he concludes, "Thus death is at work in us, but life in you" (2 Cor 4:12). Where sufferings abound for the apostle, the believers are consoled, and vice versa:

> For just as the sufferings of Christ are abundant for us, so also our consolation is abundant through Christ. If we are being afflicted, it is for your consolation and salvation; if we are being consoled,

> it is for your consolation, which you experience when you patiently endure the same sufferings that we are also suffering. Our hope for you is unshaken; for we know that as you share in our sufferings, so also you share in our consolation. (2 Cor 1: 5–7)

In conclusion, although in the eyes of the world the apostle seems an imposter, his words demonstrate that he is living, recognized, and truthful: "as sorrowful, yet always rejoicing; as poor, yet making many rich; as having nothing and yet possessing everything" (see 2 Cor 12:10). In other words, precisely when he is weak, he is strong (see 2 Cor 12:10).

We notice in these texts that the suffering is not the suffering of Paul, but that of Christ, and for this reason it is transforming and brings the consolation of the Spirit and the life of Jesus: "For just as the sufferings of Christ are abundant for us, so also our consolation is abundant through Christ" (2 Cor 1:5). In our own flesh we carry around the very "death of Christ" (see 2 Cor 4:10–11, 14); we complete "what is lacking in the sufferings of Christ" (see Col 1:24). There he finds his joy (see 2 Cor 1:24) and boasts of his infirmities (see 2 Cor 12:8–10).

Such pairs of opposites are a constant theme in the letters of Paul: life-death, curse-blessing, poverty-wealth. They refer to Jesus, but have an impact on the life of the apostle, on the relation between the apostle and the Christians, and on the relation among Christians. These opposite pairs are the structural background of the apostle's thought and style. The paradox of God who manifested himself in Jesus Christ has now become the criterion for evaluating human history and events.

Gaining access to the paschal mystery "through faith," expressed in being reconciled with God

How can an individual access this logic and put it into practice? For Paul the answer leaves no room for doubt: through faith. Faith is the way to possess this transformed life. But it is necessary to understand what faith means for Paul. I will try to summarize Paul's concept of faith as it relates to Jesus forsaken.

For Paul, the object of faith is the resurrection, that is, the power of God to transform death into life. Faith also points toward the reality in which you believe, that is, that Christ who died for our sins is now risen for our justification.[109] But faith is also — and perhaps above all — the attitude of an individual who embraces this reality, holds it to be true. How? By "letting yourself" reconcile with God.

The reconciliation accomplished by God in Christ and offered to us came about in the following way: "For our sake he made him to be sin who knew no sin, so that in him we might become the righteousness of God" (2 Cor 5:21). Quite a large message is implied in this Pauline summary: by accepting that he be made sin for us, dying on a cross — a fate reserved for the cursed of God — Jesus conceded to fill in the separation from God that had befallen us. Through his acceptance he defused sin and death along with their power. The ignominious death that Christ accepted defuses our death(s), gives us life, changes the

---

109. "In the writings of Paul, the verb *pisteuein* often signifies accepting the resurrection of Jesus as real and salvific; the noun *pistis* is sometimes used to indicate the content of the apostolic preaching." Franco Ardusso, "L'atto di Fede," *Dizionario teologico interdisciplinare* 2 (Turin: Marietti, 1977), 178.

negative signs to positive signs. In him all God's promises have really become yeses (see 2 Cor 1:20).

But the reconciliation of the world by God and its results as well as the way in which it happened are offered to us, never imposed. To enjoy them we must accept them. And accepting them means acknowledging that the Son wished to clothe himself in our sufferings, that he took our sufferings on himself (see Is. 53:4–5).

Thus Paul *pleads* with us in the name of Christ to accept: "We entreat you on behalf of Christ, be reconciled to God" (2 Cor 5:20; see Rom 5: 6–11).[110] He entreats us, because the next step is up to us; Christ has already done his part. In the name of Christ Paul entreats us not to squander the gift Christ has given us. And he knows that it is difficult to believe that Christ loved us to the point of taking up our sin and death, which separated us from God. He knows that it is difficult to "accept" that all the way to the cross Christ himself accepted the fact that we had interfered in and destroyed God's plan for creation; that Christ had accepted God's reducing him to powerlessness; that he had accepted our conduct, which would cause him to be eliminated, to be put to death. Our acceptance of what he accepted is neither a linear process, nor a foregone conclusion. Yet, in order to become the "justice of God" it is necessary for us to follow this path and let ourselves be reconciled!

If we do — and this is the amazing thing — we resemble the one upon whom the Father has bestowed all his love.

---

110. "In Christ God was reconciling the world to himself, not counting their trespasses against them, and entrusting the message of reconciliation to us. So we are ambassadors for Christ, since God is making his appeal through us; we entreat you on behalf of Christ, be reconciled to God. For our sake he made him to be sin who knew no sin, so that in him we might become the righteousness of God" (2 Cor 5:19–21).

In fact, our attitude perfectly mirrors his: Christ became obedient to the point of death—even death on a cross; and for this God exalted him (see Phil 2:8). And we, who believe in the uniqueness of this extraordinary obedience that saves us, accept that this wondrous thing (God becoming man, dying for us, being raised for us) takes place. Let us "obey" the word of salvation, which is Jesus crucified and risen. Let us try to enter into this current of love. Out of obedience he accepted to come down, and we expect to be raised up with him through obedience, because faith involves obedience (see Rom 1:5; 16:26). This is the act of faith; it is our acceptance of reconciliation with an act that parallels his. Only this act can clothe us with his dignity, liberate us. This is exactly what Paul means when he talks about dying with him in order to be raised with him (see Rom 6:4; Col 2:12; Gal 3:27). In other words, a sort of *perichoresis* takes place between the "crucified and risen Jesus and the person who receives him in faith: in faith the person dies with Christ who died on the cross (Rom 5:19) and in this death of the ego Christ crucified lives with his very own life in the believer" (see Rom 5:20).[111]

We must note that God does not require anything of the individual, but through the apostle "pleads" for believers to let themselves be reconciled because it is a free act and "the act of faith is the freest among all the acts."[112] The path of faith opened by Christ is ultimately very simple.[113]

---

111. Rossé, *La fede in San Paolo*, 153.
112. Henri de Lubac, *Paradoxes* (Paris: Editions du Livre françcais, 1946), 13.
113. In its "simplicity" this recalls what the prophet Elisha requires of Namaan the leper in order for him to be healed: wash seven times in the Jordan. It is the servants of Naaman who convince him to go through with it: "If the prophet had asked you to do something difficult, you would have done it. This is so simple and you don't want to do it!" See 2 Kings, 5:10–13.

It follows naturally that those who have let themselves be "reconciled"—and therefore have believed—gain access to revelation, salvation, justification, and holiness. For this reason Paul never grows weary of reminding us that we are saved through faith (see 2 Thes 2:13; see 1 Pt 1:5); we have life through faith for the just one shall live "by faith" (see Gal 3:11; Rom 1:17); we are justified "by faith" (see Rom 3:22, 28, 30; 4:11; 5:1; Gal 3:8–24); we are heirs "by faith" (see Rom 4:20) and children of God (see Gal 3:26). Moreover, revelation comes only "through faith" (see Rom 1:17). In other words, "through faith" we receive the Spirit, which is the object of the promise (see Gal 3:14) and Christ dwells in our hearts (see Eph 3:17). The phrases "through faith" or "by faith" can be paraphrased: "Through being voluntarily grafted into the death and resurrection of Jesus."

Hence, for Paul, faith is the attitude of someone who accepts God's design of love, the design of his wisdom and power that are revealed in Christ Jesus. It is a living assent to this design in a movement that mirrors that of Christ, who was obedient unto death and exalted above every other name. In short, it is a *perichoresis* of love between Christ and us.

Faith and the gift of the spirit

Since such faith is necessary for salvation, can it also be said to be sufficient for salvation? In the letter to the Thessalonians, where Paul's thought first arises and is expressed beyond any theological controversy, the first condition for being saved is faith. But faith is not everything. The apostle also cites hope and charity, and affirms that the word received from faith "acts" in the believers. Faith should not remain passive; the believer should "lead a life worthy of God who calls you into his own kingdom and glory"

(1 Thes 2:12), illuminated by mutual love and by bodily holiness. Yes, it is necessary to believe, but faith should blossom in holiness, charity and bodily purity.

God bestows love and holiness through his Spirit. What saves us, Paul concludes, are the Spirit of love who sanctifies us, and faith in the truth (see 2 Thes 2:13–14). In fact, in order to reach eternal glory at Christ's return, two things will be required: faith and the Spirit.

In Romans and Galatians a new terminology is introduced to address the problem of Judaizing. "Justice" and "justification" take the place of "holiness" and "sanctification." Paul is quite clear in both epistles: "For we hold that a person is justified by faith apart from works prescribed by the law" (Rom 3:28). Paul's words have an absolute value: "By what law [are human beings justified]? By that of works? No, but by the law of faith" (Rom 3:27). This means that persons are justified by faith alone.

Nevertheless, there is no contradiction, but a deep unity between justification-sanctification by faith alone and the justification-sanctification that is worked by the Spirit of love. Faith understood as the grafting into the death and resurrection of Jesus is the only source of the Spirit, whose fruits are "love, joy, peace, patience, kindness, generosity, faithfulness, and self-control" (Gal 5:22–23). Paul concludes, "If we live by the Spirit, let us also walk according to the Spirit" (Gal 5:25–26).

The Spirit moves in us when we unite ourselves to Christ, who died and rose. We die with him, but only to be raised with him to a new life (see Rom 6:4) enabling us to love and therefore accomplish the justice required by the law; that is, the justice accomplished by the one who obeys the precept of love (see Rom 13:8–10). What counts is love: "If I have all faith, so as to remove mountains, but do not have love, I am nothing" (1 Cor 13:2).

We are given saving faith by the Spirit of love. This clarifies greatly the relationship between faith and works. We are not justified by works. But if our faith is authentic we cannot but perform the works of the Spirit. "Faith creates in human beings that structure of not-being-of-self, allowing that other gift to be inserted, which is agape."[114]

Adhering to the paschal mystery means receiving yourself from God's hands

Let us take a further step. Being justified by his union with Christ who dies and is raised up, Christians will never become complacent because of their works, nor even for having allowed themselves to be reconciled. Christians accept that they are saved and justified as a free gift from the hands of God. If God had decided that we could justify ourselves by our works, we could then have boasted of them, a temptation always lurking. Paul says it quite clearly:

> He did this to show his righteousness, because in his divine forbearance he had passed over the sins previously committed. It was to prove at the present time that he himself is righteous and that he justifies the one who has faith in Jesus. Then what becomes of boasting? It is ruled out. By what law? By that of works? No, by the law of faith. (Rom 3:26–27)

Those who pretend to bring about their own supernatural destiny through their own strength boast of their works: "But the act of faith rules out this self-sufficiency more

---

114. Rosse, *La fede in San Paolo*, P. Coda - C. Hennecke (ed.), *La Fede, evento e promessa* (Rome: Città Nuova, 2000), 155–156.

than any other act, because the individual explicitly admits to his or her basic insufficiency."[115]

All those who want to be saved must recognize their own nothingness in front of God, who alone is everything. In fact, pride is an attitude of the "old man," the person outside of Christ. It is the opposite of insufficiency, because it is relies on itself. By nature faith is humble, and a Christian's life must be based on the law of humility inasmuch as it is an act of faith. Indeed, according to Paul's reasoning, it is better to boast of weaknesses (see 2 Cor 11–30 and 12:5), because if we accept those weaknesses, Christ lives in us and by so doing we encounter the Spirit of the one who raised Jesus from the dead. The apostle concludes: "Therefore I am content with weaknesses, insults, hardships, persecutions, and calamities for the sake of Christ; for whenever I am weak, then I am strong" (2 Cor 12:10). This means not that the apostle enjoys suffering, but that he says yes to it.

Living the faith (sharing in the death and resurrection of Christ), builds community

Something fundamental would be missing from this analysis without the believer's assent to or sharing in the life of Christ; that is, the communitarian, ecclesial dimension of a believer's life. The Christ who died and rose is one and the same with the Christ who lives in the Church and therefore in each of the faithful. For Paul it is the life "in Christ" that undoubtedly defines the Christian life. The term "in Christ" is repeated 164 times in Paul's writings.

---

115. Stanislaus Lyonnet, in M.-E. Boismard, 87.

For Paul, however, being "in Christ" means being in Christ's body.[116]

By accepting the paschal mystery, the believer automatically becomes part of the community of faith. This is obvious to Paul, for ethical norms stem from being "in Christ." Therefore, they cannot but be related to the relationships in the heart of the community among Christians. For Christians, being conformed to Christ means holding with the same sentiments that are "in Christ" (see Phil 2:5) and loving one another with affection as would brothers or sisters, outdoing one another in their esteem for one another (Rom 12:10) and regarding others as better than themselves (see Phil 2:3).

Since faith means sharing in the death and resurrection of Jesus, it must assume the dimension and characteristics of Christ's death-for-us and comes to fruition in life-for-others.[117] When Paul speaks of "faith in Christ" he expects us to understand that such faith generates a community of the reconciled, the forgiven; when he speaks of unity of the body we are to understand that this unity is based on each member's sharing in the death and resurrection of Jesus and Christ living in each one. "Reconciliation with God is inseparable from entrance into the fraternal unity of the Body of Christ. Membership in the brotherhood of the ecclesial body is part of the new situation created by Salvation."[118] The letter to the Galatians summarizes this succinctly: "As many of you as were baptized into Christ.... you are one [person] in Christ Jesus" (Gal 3:27–28).

---

116. See Jean-Marie Roger Tillard, *Chair de l'Eglise, chair du Christ: aux sources de l'ecclesiologie de communion* (Paris: Cerf, 1992), 15.
117. "The relationship to *the other* (Christ) is intrinsic to the Christian life. It constitutes it. But the relationship to Christ is inseparable from relationship *to others*. *The other* implies *the others*" (Tillard, 16).
118. Ibid., 18.

The letter to the Ephesians suggests the theological reasoning behind this. By dying, Jesus Christ has broken down hostility. "For he is our peace; in his flesh he has made both groups into one and has broken down the dividing wall, that is, the hostility between us" (Eph 2:14). Reconciliation with God through the one who has broken down the hostility must also include reconciliation with those who were reconciled through his blood. "The reality of the body...and its origin on the cross in the destruction of the walls of separation, provides the essential law of the Christian life: to 'imitate God' by living 'in love' as 'Christ loved us and gave himself up for us' (Eph 5:2)."[119]

Therefore the Church is constituted by what Tillard calls a "common, unique reality" of "indivisible values," a "common fund," of "common absolutes."[120] This absolute commonality is the fact of being reconciled, the active sharing in the death and resurrection of Jesus. In other words, for Paul, "living the faith means living in Jesus, in love."[121]

Faith leads to hope

Like Abraham, our father in faith, we already possess what we believe. We hope "against hope," because Jesus is risen. "For in hope we were saved" (Rom 8:24). The apostle is certain of this: "I consider that the sufferings of this present time are not worth comparing with the glory about to be revealed to us" (Rom 8:18). And "If we hope for what we do not see, we wait for it with patience" (Rom 8:25).

---

119. Ibid., 20.
120. See Ibid., 22 and 24. "The more solid and deep the common fund, the more differences the spaces for movement have and the necessary freedom for them to be expressed" (24).
121. Coda, *La fede: un introduzione*, 27.

For Paul, adhering to the paschal mystery also has an impact on creation. It is a participation in a generating—a birthing—that takes in all of creation: "For the creation waits with eager longing for the revealing of the children of God; for the creation was subjected to futility, not of its own will but by the will of the one who subjected it, in hope that the creation itself will be set free from its bondage to decay and will obtain the freedom of the glory of the children of God" (Rom 8:19–21).

For Paul, faith signifies a sharing in the paschal mystery, accessing a reality that already exists, the death and resurrection of Jesus. It is essentially a free gift of God's love that influences all of creation. Entering into Christ, into the mystery of his death and resurrection, requires obedience; it requires that the reconciliation which has already been given be allowed to come to fruition. This entering, correctly understood, cannot but lead to *agape*, to the Church. And this entering in is also an immersion, a new life. It is the essence of the life of Christians, like the water in which they were baptized.

For Paul, faith—adhering to the paschal mystery—mirrors the same movement that was in Christ as he lived his life in obedience to the Father. In Paul there is a *perichoresis* between Christ and the believer.

Chapter 5

"BELIEF" IN THE GOSPEL OF JOHN

We now turn to the Fourth Gospel to identify the content, structure, and rhythm upon which the "love for Jesus forsaken" that Chiara Lubich speaks of might be based. This is a challenging task, mainly because the Gospel of Light's complexity requires different interpretive keys to unlock the richness of its thought. Moreover, whereas many elements of Chiara Lubich's spirituality of communion, such as God love (see 1 Jn 4:16), mutual love (see Jn 15:12), and unity above all (see Jn 17) are rooted in Johannine theology, it seems that the key to unity with God and with our brothers and sisters, the choice to love Jesus forsaken, is not.

To introduce this part of the analysis we point out two noteworthy trajectories that run through the entire Gospel of John: one a dialectic line, and the other a line of unity. The first contains contrasting opposites: light-darkness, faith-unbelief, heaven-earth, knowledge-ignorance, condemnation-salvation. This axis that runs through the fourth gospel concerns the world and the relationship of those in it to the incarnation of the Word. The coming of Jesus among his own marks off the clear distinction between these mutually irreconcilable notions.

The other trajectory that runs through this Gospel is that of unity: the unity of Jesus with the Father, upon which the Gospel is based; and the unity that flows between Jesus and human beings, unity being the work of the Father and of the Son. Unlike the previous pattern, this one concerns heaven, eternal life, the love of God. Several other saving realities are related to these two main lines, like tributaries to a river: revelation, a central idea in John's gospel, flows from the incarnation of the Word and, in the final analysis, from the unity of the Father and the Son. Salvation, eternal life and faith all flow from adherence to Christ and, in the final analysis, from the unity of the Father and the Son.

The intersection of these axes is Jesus' "hour," his passion and death, which John describes as the moment freely chosen by the Son for his passing from this "world"[122] to the Father. His "hour" is also seen as the culminating moment of Jesus' love for his own (see Jn 13:1). In his death on the cross, where the passage of Jesus to the Father takes place, the fullness of the unity between the Father and the Son also takes place, their mutual glorification. The triumph of unity is manifested to the world from a cross; but as they stand before this cross, human persons also find themselves in a crisis, cornered between faith and unbelief, light and darkness, knowledge and ignorance –it requires them to take a position. Depending on this decision, a person will remain either on the axis of the dialectic or join the current of unity. This briefly describes the notion of faith and its relationship with revelation and salvation in the Fourth Gospel.

---

122. In John, the "world" is often identified with unbelief, darkness, judgment. But not always: For John, the notion of "world" does not always indicate a principle of opposition to God. John also knows a "world" that is the work of the creative Word and the place of his coming (1: 9–14; 9:5). That world is animated by God; it is the object of his project of salvation.

"Belief," passing from dialectic to unity

1. Types of belief in John

Exegetes divide the Fourth Gospel into two great sections: the Book of Signs (Chapters 1–12) and the Book of Glory (Chapters 13–21). The first section is built up through several "signs," that is, miracles and actions Jesus performs, which the author uses to "reveal" who Jesus is and to inspire faith in him. Revelation and faith are closely united.

The Jesus of John's Gospel strongly emphasizes the importance of "believing" in order to not come under judgment. But rather than accentuating judgment, condemnation, or the death of those who *do not* believe (in 3:18; 8:24; 16:11), the evangelist emphasizes instead what is reserved for those who *do* "believe in him." Jesus has not come to condemn the world, but to save it (3:17). Believing makes us sons and daughters of God (1:2), gives us eternal life (3:15; 5:24; 6:47), makes us realize God's love (3:16), satisfies our hunger (6:33), makes us accomplish the works of God (6:29), allows us to receive the Spirit (7:39) and have life beyond death (11:25–26), see the glory of God (11:40), and experience beatitude (20:29).

John always emphasizes an attitude of active "believing," a term that appears ninety-nine times under three main forms:

- *pisteuein eis*: "believe that," referring to the content of what is believed. This construction always has Christ as the object, the Son of God, who lives in communion of life with God. This construction reaches its culmination when it has for its compliment *otti ego eimi*: "believe that I am."

- *pisteuein eis*: "believe in" the name of Christ, the Son, Jesus. This construction implies a reference to the content, like *pistuein oti*, but it also implies a movement of personal adherence to Jesus.

- *pisteuein* + dative case: *pisteuein auto, pisteuein emoi*, a construction that appears ten times. This is an absolutely original construction in the New Testament, "which signifies acceptance of the self-testimony of the Son of God, in which the Father gives witness to himself. You believe "in Him" because he is the One who reveals.

This gospel, written "so that we might believe," is rich in examples of "types of believing" that help us understand the various levels of faith and unbelief, as well as the authentic faith that Jesus requires. Here are some examples.

a) The faith of the Jews and the trust of Jesus for them

John 2:23–25 states: "When he was in Jerusalem during the Passover festival, many believed in his name because they saw the signs that he was doing. But Jesus on his part would not entrust himself to them, because he knew all people and needed no one to testify about anyone; for he himself knew what was in everyone." In this case we are dealing with the faith of the Jews who "believe" in him (in his name) by seeing the signs he performs. This faith is not deep enough for Jesus, because the evangelist says that Jesus would not entrust himself to them (verse 24). Jesus performs signs so that they may believe in him, but he requires deep faith of those who receive the sign. Without this he cannot accept their belief. The faith that Jesus requires must go beyond the signs, as will be seen in the next chapter with Nicodemus.

b) The conversation with Nicodemus is the anti-sign of the lifting up on the cross (Jn 3:1–21)

Nicodemus saw and was impressed by the "signs." "Rabbi, we know that you are a teacher who has come from God; for no one can do these signs that you do apart from the presence of God" (Jn 3:2). Yet, full of his knowledge, he places himself on the same plane as Jesus, remaining within the parameters of his own judgment without opening himself to the complete newness of the rebirth brought by Jesus, as is apparent from the "we know" that opens the dialogue and because of his questioning and profound lack of understanding:

"How can anyone be born after having grown old? Can one enter a second time into the mother's womb and be born?" "How can these things be?" Jesus invites his listener to open himself to the prospect of a radical renewal, to regeneration, because authentic faith is accompanied by a rebirth from above, from the Spirit. There is an absolute need for the decisive intervention of God, a radical act like that of the parents in a birth. The mention of "the wind" — "The wind blows where it chooses, and you hear the sound of it, but you do not know where it comes from or where it goes. So it is with everyone who is born of the Spirit" (Jn 3:8) — indicates the condition in which the individual who is "born again" lives, which differs from that of the world. For this rebirth, the certain required dispositions are primarily a work of "truth." Faith presupposes a spiritual affinity with truth. This affinity with the truth is shown in a preference for the light rather than darkness, and one will acquire this preference by doing the good. "For all who do evil hate the light and do not come to the light, so that their deeds may not be exposed. But those who do what is true come to the light, so that it may be clearly seen that their deeds have been done in God" (Jn 3:20–21). Doing the truth in order to come to the light also implies recognizing oneself to be a sinner: "If you were blind, you would not have sin. But now that you say, 'We see,' your sin remains" (Jn 9:41).

Although an affinity with the truth leading to a rebirth from above (a sign of authentic faith) must distinguish those to whom Jesus can trust himself, the sign that Jesus gives for believing in him appears paradoxical. It is no longer a "miracle-sign" but a "sign beyond the sign," what might be called a "non-sign," and anti-sign: it is his testimony, his word, which is sufficient inasmuch as it is the word of a "witness." Jesus reproves Nicodemus for not believing in his own self-testimony: "Very truly, I tell you, we speak of what we know and testify to what we have seen; yet you do not receive our testimony" (Jn 3:11). Further on in the gospel it will be seen that the faith Jesus requires implies certain dispositions of a spiritual order in order to recognize the seal of the Father (Jn 6:27), the work of the Father in the works of Christ, the word of the Father in the words of Christ. A certain pre-understanding is necessary. To believe in Jesus it is necessary already to know him, already to be part of his flock. From within, the individual must be in tune with Jesus: to be from above (Jn 8:23); to be from God (Jn 8:47); to belong to the truth (Jn 18:37); to be his sheep (Jn 10:14).

Another "anti-sign" in the third chapter of John's Gospel is that of the serpent: "And just as Moses lifted up the serpent in the wilderness, so must the Son of Man be lifted up, that whoever believes in him may have eternal life" (Jn 14:15). God sent poisonous snakes to punish the Hebrews (see Num. 21:6), but thanks to the bronze serpent that Moses raised up on a pole they were saved from their deadly bites. John compares this to the lifting up of the Son of Man, with a double meaning: both the cross and the victory of the Son of Man. With the raised serpent, God revealed and manifested his love using a sign that was a cause of death, transforming the cause of death into the remedy. Likewise, in the raising up of the Son, salvation is achieved through what was lifted up and presented for all to "look upon." Only by looking upon the bronze serpent could deadly wounds be healed. The source of death itself became the source of salvation. John anticipates by analogy that looking upon Jesus lifted up on the cross is the only source of salvation.

In Chapters 2 and 3, John shows Jesus trying to move believers away from material signs in order to raise them to a different level where they will encounter Jesus in his unity with the Father. To grasp the sign of the relationship of Jesus with the Father requires an affinity for the truth and for Jesus.

c) The discourse on the bread of life and faith in the "Father's seal" (Jn 6)

Following the multiplication of the loaves the crowd chases after another sign, but Jesus reprimands them because they have not understood the true meaning of the one he has performed: "Very truly, I tell you, you are looking for me, not because you saw signs, but because you ate your fill of the loaves" (see Jn 6:26). What distinguishes the authentic faith asked for in the "bread of life" discourse is not "looking for Jesus" because he multiplied loaves of bread, but "working for the food that endures for eternal life" (see Jn 6:27).

Working means passing from an earthly food that perishes (Jn 26:27) to the knowledge of a food that gives eternal life, a passage accomplished through "believing" in the one whom God has sent (see Jn 6:29). These verses from John make it clear that the object of "belief" is acknowledging that the Father's seal is on the Son (Jn 6:27), that the Son does only what the Father wills (see Jn 6:38–40). Therefore faith is the work of the Father who draws all to the Son (Jn 6:44), and the locus of this "belief" is the relationship between Father and Son.

To those who ask for a sign, Jesus offers yet another anti-sign: himself, the living will of the Father, upon whom the Father has placed his seal, the new manna come down from heaven (see Jn 6:32).

> Everything that the Father gives me will come to me, and anyone who comes to me I will never drive away; for I have come down from heaven, not to do my own will, but the will of him who sent me. And this is the will of him who sent me, that I should lose nothing of all that he has given me, but raise it up on the last day. (Jn 6:37–39)

As in Chapter 3, here also the anti-sign is Jesus' self-testimony, his body and blood (Jn 6:30) given by the Father for the life of the world (Jn 6:33). "Believing" therefore means not being scandalized by this anti-sign, the body and the blood (Jn 6:61), not murmuring about this (Jn 6:41) but moving beyond the miracle-sign, nourishing yourself on Jesus, the bread of life, consuming his flesh and his blood. And it should be noted that here it is not the bread that becomes body as in the last supper described in the synoptic gospels, but the body and the blood that become food, bread.

The bread of life discourse summarizes the different levels of belief in Jesus in his relationship with the Father. Faith that calls for signs is insufficient: "You do not believe" (Jn 6:36). Faith in Jesus does not depend on miracle signs: "you ate food that perishes." Their unbelief becomes total when they reject the sign beyond the sign—such as the self-testimony of the one who does the Father's will; or the sign of the body and blood ("How can this man give us his flesh to eat?" [Jn 6:52]); or the sign of a challenging teaching ("This teaching is difficult; who can accept it?" [Jn 6:60]). Believing presupposes a spiritual disposition: being drawn (Jn 6:44); despite the scandal of the cross, recognizing Jesus as the one sent by the Father; recognizing him as the "Son of Man ascending to where he was before" (Jn 6:62).

John speaks of intimacy with Jesus for anyone who believes. A believer lives through Jesus, nourished with his body and his blood. This intimacy is similar to that of Jesus with the Father, since Jesus lives "because of the Father" (Jn 6:57).

d) A man blind from birth, or the movement toward perfect "belief" (Jn 9)

In Chapter 9 John presents a man blind from birth whose faith evolves until it reaches perfection. The first stage of this belief is obedience to the command to "go wash in the pool of Siloam (which means Sent)" (Jn 9:7). The second stage, after receiving his sight (Jn 9:11), consists in recognizing Jesus as a prophet (Jn 9:17). Then, in spite of everything and everyone, the man recognizes the work that has been accomplished: "One thing I do know, that though I was blind, now I see" (Jn 9:25). He declares openly that it could not have been a sinner who has healed him: "We know that God does not listen to sinners" (Jn 9:31). On the contrary, this is someone who comes from God (Jn 9:33). He is not afraid to confront Jesus' enemies, and Jesus presents him with the ultimate question: "'Do you believe in the Son of Man?' He answered, 'And who is he, sir? Tell me, so that I may believe in him.' Jesus said to him, 'You have seen him, and the one speaking with you is he.' He said, 'Lord, I believe.' And he worshiped him." (Jn 9:35–38) — a gesture of perfect belief.

The sign of the authenticity of the blind man's faith is his rebirth. He is no longer the same person, unrecognizable also in his determination to proclaim the truth according to his conscience. The sign that brings him to the faith, however, is the work that Jesus accomplishes in him, which cannot but be from God. The man blind from birth goes beyond the miracle-sign to grasp and accept the sign that Jesus is sent by God, and to receive the fullness of the revelation: "the one speaking with you is he." Jesus can entrust himself to him, and he to Jesus.

In contrast to the light of this illumination, we have the belief of the accusers, who represent those who are hostile to the revelation. They base themselves on their own self-sufficiency, on the Law about the Sabbath, on their social and religious status (Jn 9:34). The sign they expect is to know Jesus' origins, to know his concept of the Sabbath. They are incapable of recognizing Jesus as the light of the world.

e) Insufficient belief: Mary of Bethany and Thomas the apostle

When Jesus orders the stone in front of Lazarus's tomb to be taken away, Mary objects: "Lord, already there is a stench because he has been dead for four days" (Jn 11:39). Although these words are prompted by love, Mary's belief is still insufficient so Jesus asks for even more faith, an additional faith in spite of the body's decomposition : "Did I not tell you that if you believed, you would see the glory of God?" (Jn 11:40).

Following the death and resurrection of Jesus, Thomas also finds himself with insufficient faith because he wants to see and touch the signs in order to believe. Jesus says to him: "Blessed are those who have not seen and yet have come to believe" (Jn 20:29). For John, believing can begin from miracle-signs, but these serve only to set the dynamic of belief into motion, because authentic belief must necessarily be based on non-signs, such as the testimony that Jesus gives of himself regarding his relationship of oneness with the Father. The death announced in various ways by the One whom God had sent—the raising of the serpent as an image of Christ, the flesh and the blood, the cross, and the death and resurrection of Lazarus—are all non-signs. It can be clearly seen that the nearer this gospel draws to the passion, the more magnificent and eloquent the miracle-signs become and the more incredulousness grows: "Although he had performed so many signs in their presence, they did not believe in him" (Jn 12:37). The sign *par excellence* that summons authentic faith is Jesus lifted on the cross, which in and of itself is an anti-sign. An added dimension, that of reciprocity, is also found here: Jesus wants to "trust" himself to them also, and he seeks in them signs of authentic faith.

The Fourth Gospel shows an evolution, a teaching of the faith that culminates in fixing our gaze on Christ lifted on a cross as the one in whom the relationship between Father and Son is to be acknowledged. It leads to an unadorned faith, strengthened by the testimony of those who have "seen and contemplated," a faith that renders "blessed" the one who is satisfied with it and does not need to see.

2. Expressions and effects of Johannine belief

Johannine faith is a dynamic, concrete, and complex process that involves love and awareness. It is a vital event that engages individuals in the depths of their being[123] and results in a rebirth to a new way of being. John expresses this in different ways, although all contain the same elements: coming to Jesus; receiving his testimony; dwelling in him, in his word, in his love; listening to his word. "Recognition, acceptance, seeing, hearing and listening, personal contact with Christ, obedience to the Spirit, all of these converge in the process of belief."[124] Therefore belief is a true movement toward Jesus Christ that involves every dimension of a person. It is the "basic process for individuals who entrust themselves to God in Jesus Christ, who reveals himself and draws near to save them."[125]

In John's Gospel seeing and believing are connected: faith is the interpretation of what has been seen, complete adherence of one's soul to the supernatural reality that has been recognized. At the same time, faith and love are mutually implicit: "In its most essential form faith is a

---

123. See Ardusso, 178. He cites Bultmann: "For John, belief is a vital event, which engages man in the depths of his being."
124. Mollat, *Saint Jean maître spirituel*, 107.
125. Mollat, "La foi dans le quatrieme Evangile," *Lumière et Vie*, 22 (1955), 92.

loving encounter."[126] For John, faith is loving Jesus.[127] The expression "love God" never appears in John's Gospel, but it does contain the call to love Jesus, a call that is persistent. Johannine faith implies love. "Faith is realized in knowledge and in love,"[128] and is proven by observing the commandments (Jn 14:15–21). It brings a person life-long options and commitment. It is a conversion, a new birth, a break with everything that binds the individual to darkness, falsehood, and sin.

In John, revelation and faith operate in a *perichoretic* relationship: an ever-more authentic faith generates an ever-deeper revelation. Whenever an individual responds with belief to the God who reveals himself in Jesus, God responds with a new coming: "Those who love me will keep my word, and my Father will love them, and we will come to them and make our home with them" (Jn 14:23). Jesus responds to the knowledge that comes from faith and love with a further revelation: "They who have my commandments and keep them are those who love me; and those who love me will be loved by my Father, and I will love them and reveal myself to them" (Jn 14:21). Therefore, revelation and faith are part of a dynamic relationship and have as a corollary the knowledge of God, salvation, and eternal life.

a) Knowledge

Whereas for Paul belief means to benefit from the paschal mystery, for John it means to enter into the revelation of the Father that is given by Jesus, to know the Father as Jesus knows him, and this knowledge is salvation, the

---

126. Ibid., 93.
127. Rossè, *La spiritualita di communion negli scritti giovannei*, 52, 59.
128. Ibid., 50.

vision of God. In one sense, faith, even in its dimension of love, precedes knowledge, yet "believing and knowledge are one."[129]

Hence, believing in Jesus cannot be separated from knowing the relationship that unites Jesus to the Father. And so, through faith you even come to the knowledge of the Father because the Father is in Jesus and Jesus in the Father.[130]

b) Salvation that is eternal life

As John so often repeats, belief introduces the believer already into eternal life. "Those who believe in me, even though they die, will live" (Jn 11:25). "Everyone who lives and believes in me will never die" (Jn 11:26). Eternal life is John's way of expressing salvation; it does not point to a future life, as it does for Paul, but to a reality that is presently active in the believer.

In John's Gospel salvation is not merely liberation from slavery and sin, but also entering into communion with God. The terms "salvation," "eternal life," and "knowledge" all refer to communion with God. Similar expressions include: "may have eternal life," "eternal life," "become children of God," "make you free," "In my Father's house there are many dwelling-places."[131]

It becomes clear that from the cross there shines forth the object of revelation, the unity of the Father and Son. There the connection between believing and loving is made evident. The full dimension of revelation is revealed as a gift of God — faith, complete acceptance by the individual believer, and salvation as a further gift on the side of God.

---

129. Mollat, *La foi dans le quatrieme Evangile*, 95.
130. Ibid., 97.
131. Mollat, *Saint Jean, maître spiritual*, 62.

Since believing is a rebirth, a new life like the one received at natural birth, it moves one from a state of fragmentation to oneness, from darkness to light, from opposition to unity with God, oneself, and others.

Let us now try to understand more deeply and concretely how faith inserts itself into the unity of the Father and the Son and the Holy Spirit; that is, in the eternal life.

Belief places the believer in Jesus' hour, when he returns to the Father

a) Jesus' hour, his return to the Father, the place where love between Father and Son can be found

In the lifting up on the cross there takes place a parting of the waters — the parting of faith and incredulity, of light and darkness. It is also the moment of Jesus' parting out of love, for the Father and the glorification, as this verse clearly states: "Now before the festival of the Passover, Jesus knew that his hour had come to depart from this world and go to the Father. Having loved his own who were in the world, he loved them to the end" (Jn 13:1). The lifting up and the hour share the same deep meaning: the loving return of Jesus to the Father.

The central theme of John's Gospel is unity. This is expressed in Jesus' journey from and to the Father. Although the term is not Johannine, this journey has been called the return of Jesus to the Father; exegetes agree, however, on the general importance of this return in the Fourth Gospel.

Jesus goes forth from the Father in order to return to him and, within the interval, accomplish the work of the one who sent him, which is to keep with him the ones who have been given to him by the Father (see Jn 6:39; 17:2;

18:9). Going forth from and returning to the Father are the two poles of a single movement: "The going forth is the returning," says von Balthasar.[132]

Jesus' return to the Father can take place only on the cross. Just as in the synoptic gospels, also in John's Jesus *had* to die ..."to gather into one the dispersed children of God" (Jn 11:51–52). But "How can you say that the Son of Man must be lifted up?" (Jn 12:34). In fact, however, Jesus returns to the Father as the Son of Man with his humanity.

By going forth from the Father, the Son assumes a place and existence inside creation in order to accomplish in the flesh, within human existence, the eternal movement in which he lives in his eternal existence, the movement of the Son toward the Father, accomplishing it with us. He turns toward the Father from within his human state and transcends the distance between flesh and spirit, between God and man, which necessarily happens through the cross.

Nevertheless, this return remains the work of the Father and the Son — reciprocal glorification, reciprocal gift. For this reason John sees the passion of Jesus as his glorification, his royal enthronement; the passage that takes place on the cross appears as his triumph.[133] Through his death, Jesus glorifies the Father and, through the resurrection, the Father glorifies the Son (see Jn 17:1–5). Nothing in the Fourth Gospel resembles the abandonment of Jesus mentioned in Mark and Matthew; however, by showing the passion as the fullness of unity between Father and Son, the return of the Son to the Father, Johannine theology brings out the genuine meaning of the abandonment.

---

132. Hans Urs von Balthasar, *Le cœur du monde* (Paris: Desclée De Brouwer, 1953), 29.
133. Being "raised up on the cross" means to be crowned. See Gerard Rossé, *The Spirituality of Communion, A New Approach to the Johannine Writings* (Hyde Park: NY, New City Press, 1998), 28.

The early tradition, which is accepted by Mark and Matthew, sees Jesus dying in isolation and expressing his sense of abandonment by God. The Fourth Gospel, on the other hand, sees the cross as the moment that sheds the clearest light on the oneness of Jesus with the Father. Is John then contradicting the early Christian tradition? No, he is in fact simply explaining to the reader the true meaning of Jesus' death as seen by faith: This death, this immense loneliness is in reality the crowning point of the revelation of God, the point at which the Son shows his supreme oneness with the Father.[134]

In John's Gospel Jesus' death is resurrection. "If John reinterprets the crucifixion so it becomes part of Jesus' glorification, he dramatizes the resurrection so that it is obviously part of the ascension. Jesus is lifted up on the cross; he is raised up from the dead; and he goes up to the Father—all as part of one action and one 'hour.'"[135] The Johannine vision of Jesus' death as glorification, therefore, in no way decreases the realism of the passion and death.

b) Adhering in faith to Jesus lifted up on the cross

Jesus' being lifted up in his hour is the way God has chosen to express his love, as Jesus explains to Nicodemus: "For God so loved the world that he gave his only Son, so that everyone who believes in him may not perish but have eternal life" (Jn 3:16). In this is manifested not only the

---

134. Ibid; 30.
135. Raymond E. Brown, *The Gospel According to John* (Garden City, NY: Doubleday, 1970), 1013–1014.

love of the Son for the Father, but also that of the Father for the Son and for the world.

We must believe in order to be inserted into this dynamic of love, and must accept what God wishes to express so lovingly in it. Such belief is eternal life. Why? In 3:16, John sums up three dimensions of God's love for the world: the revelation of love; believing in the love that is revealed in this manner; and the experience of salvation, eternal life.

He also links these dimensions: the revelation of love becomes salvation and eternal life for the one who believes. Here, believing clearly means *looking*. The object of this belief is God, that is, Jesus lifted up, the dead and glorified Jesus upon whom we *look* and see as the mutual giving of the Father and Son. Believing therefore implies accepting the gift God gives. Belief is recognizing that Jesus and the Father are one; it is recognizing that on the cross Jesus returns to the Father; and it is accepting totally the manner in which this happens, the cross. It is recognizing that the resurrection is implied in the crucifixion. Belief is looking at an apparently negative sign and accepting its real and positive sense, recognizing a divine presence in it. It also means perceiving the meaning of a non-sign. At the foot of the cross the beloved disciple solemnly testifies that he *saw* blood and water flow from Jesus' side. This testimony calls the disciple to full faith. Thus "the gazing on the One who was pierced" acknowledges in Jesus an inexhaustible source of life for believers.[136] Believing therefore means coming to the awareness that this is a gift of God and wanting to reach full enjoyment of this gift.

Only by understanding faith in this way can the apparent tautology of verse 3:18b be understood: "But those who

---

136. Xavier Léon-Dufour, *Lettura dell'evangelo secondo Giovanni*, (Cinisello Balsamo: Paoline, 1990), 226–227.

do not believe are condemned already, because they have not believed in the name of the only Son of God." This sentence only makes sense if belief means enjoyment of the love Jesus has given us.

c) Further Reflection on Sharing in the Gift of God

In addition to seeing and perceiving the meaning of the non-sign, there is another way for the disciple to enjoy the mutual gift of the Father and of the Son on the cross. Jesus returns to the Father with all those whom the Father has given to him: "Everything that the Father gives to me will come to me; and anyone who comes to me I will never drive away. ...And this is the will of him who sent me; that I should lose nothing of all that he has given me, but raise it up on the last day" (Jn 6:37, 39). Therefore, Jesus is not alone in his return to the Father; what is more, he can plead our cause. This is the sense of Chapter 17: "Holy Father, protect them in your name that you have given me, so that they may be one, as we are one." "Father, I desire that those also, whom you have given me, may be with me where I am..." (Jn 17:11, 21, 24). Moreover, he goes to the Father to prepare a place for them (see Jn 14:2) and to send them the Paraclete (Jn 16:7).

Now it is up to the disciples to be united to him. John gives several examples of this bond: being united in mutual understanding, like sheep with their shepherd (see Jn 10:14); in lifeblood, like the branches and their vine (see Jn 15: 4–6). Even more: in his return journey to the Father the disciples are united to Jesus as to a path that is the source of truth and life (see Jn 14:6). Therefore Jesus' return to the Father on the cross is *the* way for the disciples: "I am the way" (Jn 14:6). The disciple can draw full benefit from the passing of Jesus to the Father on the cross by being in Jesus-the-Way and following in his path.

The way of Jesus manifested in his death is nothing but love toward the Father and love from the Father. Similarly, with their gaze fixed on the cross, disciples must enter into this logic of love, into a concrete, fundamental, and total commitment of self to Jesus Christ. This is what Jesus requires of his disciples as the seal and fulfillment of their faith: "If you love me" and "Do you love me?" Once the believer has entered into this mystery, he or she is invited to draw from it unendingly: "and let the one who believes in me drink" (see Jn 7:37–38).

In addition, the disciple can follow the path of unity between the Father and the Son by eating the Son's flesh and drinking his blood. Indeed, the disciple's adherence to the passion of Jesus is so intimate that he or she can eat the very flesh and drink the very blood of Jesus. In summary, adhering to Jesus is a loving encounter. The believer who is inserted into Jesus-the-Way passes, like Jesus, from death to life.

In the farewell discourse (Chapters 13–17), Jesus no longer addresses the Jews in order to explain what it means to believe in him. He turns to his disciples, his friends, the believers who recognize the link between faith and love. This discourse is introduced by the washing of feet, which in the synoptic gospels is comparable to the institution of the Eucharist. Allowing Jesus to wash your feet means to have a share with him (Jn 13:9), and Peter clearly understands this (Jn 13:10). But it also means entering into the logic of washing each other's feet (see Jn 13:14), a logic that Jesus solemnly establishes with his new commandment (Jn 13:34). Belief involves following his commandments, listening to his word. The commandment of love entails passing from death to life, a passing which resembles that of the Son to the Father: "We know that we have passed from death to life because we love one another" (1 Jn 3:14).

Thus in John's Gospel belief can be defined as recognizing the cross of Jesus as his Passover to the Father out of love and for the mutual glorification of Father and Son. It involves entering out of love into a dynamic that is similar to his: passing from perishable food to the heavenly food (the dead and risen Jesus); passing from death to life by living according to the commandment of reciprocal love.

Believing is love for Jesus as he leaves this world, returns to the Father, remaining in him and with him. Through faith, believers take possession of the gift that the Father gives them in Jesus, and of the gift that Jesus gives by accomplishing the work of the Father. It is nothing more than a gift, the gift of the Father and of the Son, into whom we enter and accept. It is a gift that animates us with the "same dynamism that had led Jesus to offer the gift of his life to accomplish the will of the Father and to love humankind."[137]

Christ loved his own "to the end" (Jn 13:1). Believers accomplish the same step through faith. Christ says to the Father: "Now I am coming to you" (see Jn 17:13). Believers say to the Father and to Christ: "I am coming to you." "I sanctify myself so that they may be sanctified" (see Jn 17:19). Believers go to Christ together with the brothers and sisters they love and serve. There is a complete harmony between perfect belief and love.

The movement in Johannine faith is revealed ever more clearly as a response to a counter-movement that preceded it, a motion that stems from the intimate core of God's life

---

137. L. Cilia, "La morte di Gesù e l'unità degli uomini," in Rossé, *La spiritualità di comunione negli scritti giovannei*, 36.

to reach humankind in Jesus and to draw humankind into the unity of the Father and the Son.[138]

Mother of Jesus, icon of belief

In the Gospel of John, Jesus' mother appears twice: at the wedding feast of Cana and at the foot of the cross.

At Cana, when the water is changed into wine, she anticipates Jesus' hour, affliction changing to joy. Her believing in his power to transform water to wine foreshadows that hour. The wedding in Cana sheds light on how the hour, Jesus' death and resurrection, is the moment in which realities change sign.

In Jn 19:25–27 Mary is presented as the icon of Abraham, the father of all believers, who is willing to sacrifice his son (see Gn 22:3). As in the Annunciation (see Lk 1:45) and at Cana, where Mary believed, she continues to play a pioneering role at the moment when the hour arrives, when Jesus entrusts the beloved disciple to her. Jesus has taken us with him to place us in him, the Way to the Father; just so, he asks Mary to take on new sons and daughters. Mary is the first believer, intimately linked to the Son, that is, the first to walk along the Way that is her Son. In the same way each of us, inasmuch as we are children of Mary, is invited to keep our brothers and sisters with us, to unite with them as Jesus had done, and to pass with them from this world to the Father. And this can only be done on the cross: "Unless a grain of wheat falls into the earth and dies, it remains just a single grain; but if it dies, it bears much fruit" (Jn 12:24). Thus, authentic belief, being in an intimate union with the Son who has been welcomed as the one sent by the Father, consists in retracing the movement of the Son who returns

---

138. Mollat, *La foi dans le quatrième Évangile*, 7.

to the Father by being raised up on the cross, the sign of the perfect unity with the Father and, for those who do not believe, the anti-sign *par excellence*.

Believing means *being in Jesus-the-Way*, taking the step that he took on the cross, with our gaze fixed on him, a gaze that leads to being absorbed into him, being nourished on him—in answer to his love. Believing is therefore a passover; it is paschal gratitude and joy. The faith process reveals the immanence of Christ's life in believers, and believers' life in Christ. Nevertheless, the concrete reality of Johannine faith is dramatic, as the man blind from birth testifies with his witness. Faith, inscribed within the great clash between light and darkness, takes place at the level of freedom and decision. The drama of faith reflects the distance between a divine God who offers the gift of salvation for all and an earthly humankind who neither expect nor desire such a gift. The object, structure, motivation, and dynamic process of faith rests on a non-sign, and so must be a personal and radical choice focused on the unity of the Father and Son. From a Johannine perspective, such unity gives rise to the hatred for Jesus that leads to his condemnation and death.

Conclusion

In Paul we saw the importance of a radical and meaningful choice of the dead and risen Christ; the obedience of faith manifested in being reconciled with Christ, mirroring Christ's obedience to his Father; and an emphasis upon the fruits of love and building up the Church when we are grafted in Christ.

In John, *belief* is a *crisis*, an unavoidable decision to follow the path of faith. This decision is accomplished in Jesus' hour, his cross. There his unity with the Father shines forth, and from it he returns to the Father with us. Jesus' hour compels a decision; it distinguishes between faith and disbelief, light and darkness, knowledge and ignorance, salvation and condemnation. Concretely, choosing Jesus in his hour—the locus of faith, light, knowledge, salvation—means in our sufferings, whatever they may be, fixing our gaze on him, responding to his love that has already taken them up, assimilating his body and blood as food and drink. Thus it means passing from suffering to love, from death to life. Ultimately, it coincides with the commitment to follow his commands, especially that of mutual love.

Faith is a response to the extraordinary call to follow a path of glory and suffering, just like the Son who brings us into the glory of the children of God. Faith is a response to a summons beyond our imagination: to be in Jesus-the-Way. *Loving Jesus forsaken* thus is revealed to be a complex and dynamic activity analogous to the complex and dynamic act of faith.

Chiara seldom uses the word "faith." Usually, she speaks of love that creates community, but beneath her entire life and thinking lies the reality of faith. Paul's expression "by faith," which signifies a vital adherence to God's loving design and its salvific effects of justification and filiation, is analogous to Chiara's adherence to "love for Jesus crucified and forsaken" and its effects. The object, structure and process of John's statement "whoever believes in him" is analogous to the object, structure, and process of Chiara's "whoever loves him abandoned."

Paul comes to the dead and risen Christ through faith, and John through belief. For Chiara, a person enters into the knowledge and love of Christ by loving him in the mystery of his abandonment by the Father. By being united to him, you enter into a new understanding of reality. In Paul, opposites are put together again in unity. Poverty and wealth, loss and gain, emptying and glory become the same. Similarly for Chiara, a divine alchemy transforms suffering into love, revealing the hidden law of love.

Paul claims that *by faith* we are sons and daughters, saved and justified. Chiara echoes this claim, saying that through our love for the forsaken Jesus, the risen Lord enters us in triumph. This might seem excessive, but if Christ became sin, then it is not so strange that Paul could say "I could wish that I myself were accursed ... for the sake of my own people, my kindred according to the flesh" (Rom 9:3). And for anyone who would imitate Jesus forsaken's style of love, Chiara's attitude is logical:

At every mistake my brother makes, I ask pardon of the Father as if it were my own failing, and it is mine because my own love takes possession of it. This is how I am Jesus. And I am Jesus forsaken always before the Father as sin and as the greatest act of love toward my brothers and, therefore, toward the Father.[139]

John presents a Christ who in his death is already risen, where the tragedy lies not in the pain, but in the darkness, the judgment, the unbelief. Chiara echoes this idea, underscoring the need to go beyond the wound, affirming that the transformation of suffering into love has already happened. John notes the anti-sign of the raised serpent as the sign of our faith and therefore of our salvation. In the same fashion, Chiara points out the presence of Christ in suffering, in which the meaning of reality is perceived, the negative becoming positive.

---

139. In Hubertus Blaumeiser, "Attraverso la trasparenza del nostro nulla," *Nuova Umanità*, 120 (1998), 675.

For Christians to share in the life of Christ they must live for others and build up the community from a paschal perspective. For Paul, conforming oneself to Christ means sharing the same sentiments that are in Christ Jesus (see Phil 2:5), that is, *kenosis*; and for John, passing from death to life, which is *faith* in the Son, is accomplished by loving the brothers and sisters; and Chiara asserts: "Let us seek the suffering offered by the will of God ...*that* will of God which is mutual love, the new commandment, the pearl of the gospel!"[140]

For Paul, faith and life in the Spirit are joined; for John faith and love are one. Paul's term *in Christ* and in John's *having eternal life* sum up the fruits of faith succinctly. The same is true with Chiara's love for Jesus forsaken.

Chiara sees love for Jesus forsaken deeply rooted in scripture. By loving Jesus forsaken and making him be loved, Chiara lived what the Scripture means by *faith*, and led her brothers and sisters to live its complexity and richness. In the spirituality of Chiara Lubich and in scripture, Christians — especially those called to the spirituality of unity — can verify the genuineness of their love for Jesus crucified and forsaken. With Paul, they can ask whether their life is centered on the mystery of Christ and whether, with the gift of the Spirit, love for Jesus forsaken draws them into the entire mystery of Christ, from the incarnation to the ascension. Or are they merely seeking a way to overcome suffering? They can ask whether they boast only of their weaknesses; whether they are "just" because of their works or because of their love for Jesus forsaken; whether they are grateful and happy to *let themselves be reconciled* and remain always in awe of God, who has given them the gift of sharing in his Son's life of obedience. With John

---

140. Lubich, *The Cry*, 41.

they can ask whether they realize that they must return completely in heart, mind and spirit—a Passover from this world—to Jesus, intimately united to him, keeping with them *the ones he has given them.*

Part 3

A FEW CONSIDERATIONS ON THE ACT OF FAITH

If faith is a sharing in the paschal mystery, it is necessary to consider the nature of the act of faith. I will do this by examining several elements of *love for Jesus forsaken* more deeply from another perspective, and focusing on the dimensions of the act of faith.

Faith is not mere confidence in being saved, but *life* in Christ, something real, something based on a true fact: the death and resurrection of Jesus. It is not just a function, but an act of love for a Person. Faith is not something we have, but our *sharing in* the mystery of a Christ who died and is risen. Although a lived experience cannot be divided into components, an act of *believing* consists not in the clear and conscious adherence to a creed (although such adherence is certainly necessary), but in a *sharing in* the death and resurrection of Christ.

Chapter 6

THE ACT OF FAITH

The life of faith unfolds upon a landscape of covenant and love

Like an act of faith, Chiara's choice of Jesus forsaken unfolds against the backdrop of a covenant, of reciprocity. Its fundamental elements are response to and acceptance of the revelation of God's love, especially his having made himself one with us. Faith is a response to this good news. The radicality of the choice of Jesus forsaken corresponds to the radicality of God's love manifested in Jesus, a relationship of symmetry between the individual and God. Chiara expresses this in her prayer: *Grant me to love You as You love me.*[141]

The loving response from human persons reflects God's love. The relationship between God and humankind is a covenant, made forever. It is no coincidence that from its very first line Chiara's most important text on love for Jesus forsaken speaks explicitly of a spousal relationship, a covenant.[142] Although she never studied theology or the nature of the covenant, with her *sensus fidei* (sense of the faith) Chiara places herself at a spousal level, at the level of a covenant, which is a level of equality.

---

141. See pg. 40.
142. Lubich, *The Cry*, 61.

I have only one Spouse contains a tacit covenant proposal on the part of God. The text can even be read as the yes to a covenant proposal from the one who has espoused humankind, singularly and forever. During the illuminative period of 1949, Chiara came to understand, as she herself said, "We also understood better many truths of the faith, particularly who Jesus forsaken was for humanity and for creation—he who recapitulated all things in Himself."[143] Her *I have only one Spouse* presents the delicate countermelody of the Spouse, a declaration of love to which the bride responds with a solemn yes to the covenant that Jesus forsaken offered, even can be said to have already been consummated. Chiara chooses Jesus forsaken as her spouse because he himself has chosen to espouse humanity, even with its inconsistencies. And Chiara suggests that he has espoused it all the way to the depths of its anguish and abandonment, in all its sin and hell. Faith is a spousal response. Through faith, believers live out the covenant in a way that mirrors the way Christ does.

Loving Jesus forsaken simply means following the same path that he took. He came to accompany us in every suffering, even that of hell. In every experience of suffering we can encounter him. Jesus, even though he was in the form of God, did not regard equality with God as something to be exploited; he became obedient, even to death on a cross (see Phil 2:8). Like him, we also should renounce our self-sufficiency and recognize that in every sorrowful event, whether personal or of the world, he holds out his arms to us. It is a most noble request that he makes of us, even giving us the possibility of being the first to love him with a love that resembles his. It is not surprising, then, that Chiara speaks of consoling him, being his vineyard, giving him

---

143. Ibid., 60–61.

the satisfaction of seeing the fruits of his abandonment. These expressions are not devotional, but theological.

The paschal mystery is an *eternal covenant* in which Jesus has espoused humanity. Responding to this covenant means allowing ourselves to reciprocate what he has done for us, to espouse Jesus crucified and forsaken, to retrace the Son's path. This is the itinerary of faith. Espousing Jesus forsaken fulfills the words of Jeremiah: "But this is the covenant that I will make with the house of Israel after those days, says the LORD: I will put my law within them, and I will write it on their hearts...they shall all know me, from the least of them to the greatest" (Jer 31:33–34). God's law is Trinitarian love, the love manifested in Jesus forsaken, the love that loves and is loved in return, the love that means divinization.

Jesus became us so that we would become him. God follows the logic of the covenant to the very end; he is perfectly faithful. The very fact that God speaks in Jesus forsaken is salvific. Here the Word becomes an inclined plane, reaching all the way down to the lowest. The Word can be applied in every situation. Covenants are contracts between equals, or between parties who become equals through the covenant. Within the framework of covenant, a response in faith places us in a partnership with God at his level, the level of Jesus. In its pure form this covenant is expressed in love for Jesus forsaken, through whom we arrive at the resurrection.

Humankind's lofty call reflects God's creative action, all the way to the "new heavens" and "new earth." Humanity is called to "help God,"[144] to be God's covenant partner. Without our loving response, God cannot deal with us as

---

144. See *Etty Hillesum: An Interrupted Life, the Diaries 1941–1943 and Letters from Westerbork* (New York: Holt, 1996).

equals, and the folly of God's love consists in wishing to make humankind his equal. God humbly awaits a response, and human beings respond by sharing in the dynamic of death and resurrection.

God submits to the will of human beings. Human beings comfort God; by taking full advantage of the abandonment, they say to God that creation *was* and is *good*. This is a complete response, a faith response. In Christ, God has made himself our servant by taking the last place. In faith we can relive Christ in the dynamic of the gift. In giving himself he received himself as a gift in the resurrection; likewise, we can let ourselves to be generated and receive ourselves as a gift by giving up *having*, which only gives an illusion of being. By loving Jesus forsaken we relive his abandonment in a way that mirrors his: his *kenosis*, his having come to take us with him, the loss of God, his new creation. By *losing* God we receive a revelation of who God is.

Faith unfolds upon a landscape of revelation and knowledge

Loving Jesus forsaken inserts us into a dynamic that takes us from one revelation to another, from one knowledge to another. Chiara's adherence to the word of revelation, Jesus forsaken, brought her and her companions new understanding.

From the first revelation of *Jesus forsaken*, Chiara adhered to a word because it was Word of God, but she was also adhering to the content of that Word, which included scandal, folly, the apparent contradiction of any *rational* idea about God. She did not reconcile these two contradictory terms in an artificial way by reducing one to the other. She accepted both, coining an expression that seems to contain quite a contradiction in itself: *Jesus forsaken*. She remained in the contradiction out of humble acceptance of the revelation. This acceptance provoked a new immediate understanding: this suffering is the maximum of love.

This new understanding is perfectly rational because two things that seem to be in opposition to one another—God's love (We are personally and immensely loved by God[145]) and God's abandonment—are reconciled; God's ultimate suffering is God's greatest love. In love faith is made clear: God's love, rather than falling to pieces, deepens. Hence, the revealed Word is love not only because it is a word of revelation, but also because of what it contains. Jesus forsaken is the revelation of God who is love. It is the same dynamic as the revelation of God-Love that prompted Chiara to respond by being love. Now, the revelation of Jesus forsaken, [God's] love *revealed*, urges her to value personal suffering as an expression of love for him. Reliving Jesus forsaken-revealed requires losing one's personal idea of God and being open to an unthought-of revelation. Jesus forsaken contradicts the idea of a God *ex machina* and leads to the idea of God who is totally other. When loved, Jesus forsaken reveals who God is: God is the one of whom it can never be said: he is this or that, for in the abandonment, any possible idea of him falls to dust so as to open onto the total otherness, the transcendence of God.

Jesus forsaken lived out God's *kenosis* to reveal who God is. Reliving Jesus forsaken means passing through a *kenosis* of the mind in order to accept the contradiction that opens us to the living God who is love. Whenever we welcome Jesus forsaken in any suffering, we lose the certainty of life that brings joy and happiness in order to share in his lot. We entrust ourselves to a love that we do not see, but then

---

145. Chiara Lubich, *Essential Writings*, 338.

enter into a new relation with love: our heart opens upon God and upon our brothers and sisters. We relive his self-emptying of the wealth of a relationship that made us feel alive and reassured, in order to be nothing but love. This *kenosis* of the heart allows the reception of divine love.

Faith unfolds upon a landscape of divine presence

The reality of *presence* is quite strong in Chiara Lubich's spirituality: the presence of Christ manifested in our neighbor; the sacrament of Christ, the Eucharist; the Word of God; and mutual love. This presence, sometimes manifested through an absence, is a fruit of the risen Lord. It is the paschal mystery at work in the world, much more real than what meets the eye. Through his death Christ has drawn everything into the life of God—the *redemption was full and overflowing*, Chiara states.[146] The paschal mystery is God's final word to the world, the new creation.

Jesus crucified and forsaken took everything upon himself; because he became sin he is present everywhere, even where we would never think to find him. There is no situation that he has not known and transformed through his resurrection. He precedes us in any situation that could befall us. In him heaven and earth come together, the uncreated and the created, as Chiara says: "In him is the whole of paradise with the Trinity and the whole of the earth with humanity."[147] Recognizing the presence of Jesus forsaken in an experience of suffering means to affirm tacitly that he, abandoned and risen, is beyond space and time. It means recognizing that eschatology penetrates every fiber of our being because Christ is risen.

---

146. Ibid., 94.
147. See Lubich, *The Cry*, 61.

Chapter 6 The Act Of Faith   109

What Chiara refers to as *alchemy*, the transformation of suffering into love, Teilhard de Chardin refers to as *transformation*[148]; Benedict XVI *nuclear fission*[149] and *the greatest mutation*,[150] referring to a term used in the theory of evolution. Chiara's phrase, *suffering is Jesus forsaken*, signifies that the paschal mystery influences all creation; that it is the deepest substance of creation; that it renews the universe

---

148. In the preface of a book in which are gathered the notes written by his cousin during her life full of serious illnesses, Chardin writes: "O Marguerite my sister, while I, given soul and body to the positive forces of the universe, was wandering over continents and oceans, my whole being passionately taken up in watching the rise of all the earth's tints and shades, you lay motionless, stretched out on your bed of sickness; silently, deep within yourself, you were transforming into light the world's most grievous shadows." Ursula King, *Spirit of Fire: The Life and Vision of Teilhard de Chardin* (Maryknoll, NY: Orbis Books, 1996), 162.
149. "Since this act transmutes death into love, death as such is already conquered from within, the Resurrection is already present in it. Death is, so to speak, mortally wounded, so that it can no longer have the last word. To use an image well known to us today, this is like inducing nuclear fission in the very heart of being — the victory of love over hatred, the victory of love over death. Only this intimate explosion of good conquering evil can then trigger off the series of transformations that little by little will change the world.
    All other changes remain superficial and cannot save. For this reason we speak of redemption: what had to happen at the most intimate level has indeed happened, and we can enter into its dynamic." Homily, August 21, 2005, http://www.vatican.va/holy_father/benedict_xvi/homilies/2005/documents/hf_ben-xvi_hom_20050821_20th-world-youth-day_en.html.
150. "If we may borrow the language of the theory of evolution, it [the Resurrection] is the greatest 'mutation,' absolutely the most crucial leap into a totally new dimension that there has ever been in the long history of life and its development: a leap into a completely new order which does concern us, and concerns the whole of history." Easter Vigil Homily, April 15, 2006, http://www.vatican.va/holy_father/benedict_xvi/homilies/2006/documents/hf_ben-xvi_hom_20060415_veglia-pasquale_en.html.

and that beneath any suffering lies the resurrection, already at work, the new creation already underway.

The world we live in is moving toward an eschatological reality *yet to come*, but *already* at work within the tragedy of existence. By loving Jesus forsaken, we can live in this *already* and *not yet*. Through loving Jesus forsaken, we can be enveloped in the dynamic of Trinitarian love described succinctly by St. Paul: "For the love of Christ urges us on, because we are convinced that one has died for all; therefore all have died" (2 Cor 5:14).

By participating in this dynamic, by loving Jesus forsaken, we contribute to the new creation. Loving Jesus forsaken sets free the human-divine energy of the risen Lord; it lifts a veil that had covered what has already been redeemed, what has already been raised; it deciphers a language that seems inscrutable, restoring its total sense and meaning. This love is a collaboration in the new creation; suffering and pain are Jesus, the Son, his presence deciphered with love. We become active in the new creation, giving things their true meaning. All other changes are superficial and cannot save. This is why we speak of redemption: what we needed most deeply has happened, and we can be drawn into this dynamic. Faith must be understood as a kind of *perichoresis*, a mutual indwelling of believer and word of God. A word is communicated and the believer hears it, obeys, loves; this new awareness leads to yet another, deeper listening, a cycle that repeats infinitely. Faith is the interweaving of knowledge and love, faith and obedience. Faith is resting in the paschal mystery; it is communion with Christ; it is being another Christ; it is *acting like Jesus on earth*. Faith is knowledge, communion, human growth, divinization, and salvation.

Faith unfolds in a sacramental and especially Eucharistic framework of communion and dialogue among brothers and sisters

Faith has a sacramental dimension, and the sacrament *par excellence* is the crucified and risen Christ. All other sacraments, from Baptism to the Anointing of the Sick, have meaning only in relation to him. When in their everyday life believers share in the death and resurrection of Christ; when they proclaim what water and Word stand for in baptism; when they embrace Jesus crucified and forsaken and experience the anointing of the Holy Spirit, the gift of the risen Christ; when they live the Eucharist as the daily sharing in the sacrifice of his body and blood; when they live the priesthood, which includes the royal priesthood, as the offering of self for the world and the transformation of the cosmos; then the life of sacrament and of faith are intimately joined in a *perichoretic* relationship.

As signs, sacraments offer to the senses what already exists in those who love Jesus crucified and forsaken. When celebrated in the assembly, this reality reinforces the faith, nourishes it, and expresses it. In the sacraments, the life of love for Jesus forsaken takes on an ecclesial and universal dimension. They are the seals of its authenticity, the indicators that all of this is always and only pure gift. Moreover, faith unfolds within a landscape where differences come together in unity: faith and reason and folly; freedom and obedience; knowledge and experience; faith and love; activity and passivity. In faith opposites exist in a new synthesis.

As a sharing in the paschal mystery, faith also generates norms for living and a lifestyle that can be summarized in the Augustinian precept: Love and do what you will. Indeed, this faith is lived in a mutual indwelling with Christ, an imitation of the love of Christ, which is death and life, at the same time being and non-being. Every law is fulfilled when we love everyone. So faith unfolds within the dimension of communion with brothers and sisters. Faith , therefore, can extend beyond the boundaries of the Church. The difference between a believer and a non-believer is the concrete experience of fixing one's gaze on the suffering lived by the forsaken and risen Lord in order to provide a remedy, and recognizing in each brother or sister a small sufferer who is similar to Jesus. This is far more than intellectual adherence to any creed or an external practice of worship. With such an understanding of faith, concrete and fruitful dialogue with persons of other religions, as well as with persons of no religious faith, is possible.

Today, humankind's most pressing problem is the relation between individual and community. How are these two dimensions of human life to be reconciled? Further analysis would show that without recognizing a transcendent being that we can call God—that is, expressed or unexpressed faith—these two dimensions are incompatible. When understood as a sharing in the paschal mystery, faith cannot but bear fruit in life-for-others. Faith generates a going out of oneself to generate a community, composing in harmony the relation between individual and community that must always be rebuilt. This relation between individual and community is founded on the passage from death to life, from death of the ego to the life of an "us" where the ego finds its full breadth and freedom.

This is the faith that the Son of Man hopes to find when he returns to the earth: "And yet, when the Son of Man does come, will he find faith on earth?"(Lk 18:8).

NEW CITY PRESS
of the Focolare
Hyde Park, New York

New City Press is one of more than 20 publishing houses sponsored by the Focolare, a movement founded by Chiara Lubich to help bring about the realization of Jesus' prayer: "That all may be one" (John 17:21). In view of that goal, New City Press publishes books and resources that enrich the lives of people and help all to strive toward the unity of the entire human family. We are a member of the Association of Catholic Publishers.

Further Reading

¿Por Que Me Has Abandonado? Chiara Lubich		950-586-130-3	$17.50
5 Steps to Facing Suffering Geraldine Guadagno			
	paperback	978-1-56548-502-0	$4.95
	e-book	978-1-56548-570-9	$3.95
The Cry of Jesus Crucified and Forsaken Chiara Lubich			
		978-1-56548-159-6	$11.95
Early Letters Chiara Lubich		978-1-56548-432-0	$15.95
Essential Writings: Spirituality, Dialogue, Culture Chiara Lubich			
	paperback	978-1-56548-259-3	$24.95
	e-book	978-1-56548-347-7	$9.95
Introduction to the Abba School Abba School		978-1-56548-176-3	$11.95
Jesus: The Heart of His Message Chiara Lubich			
	paperback	978-1-56548-090-2	$8.95
	e-book	978-1-56548-090-2	$4.99
Only at Night We See the Stars Chiara Lubich		978-1-56548-158-9	$11.95

Periodicals
Living City Magazine,
www.livingcitymagazine.com

Scan to join our mailing list for discounts and promotions
or go to
www.newcitypress.com
and click on "join our email list."

www.ingramcontent.com/pod-product-compliance
Lightning Source LLC
LaVergne TN
LVHW051645080426
835511LV00016B/2496